THE GIANT SIGHT WORD WORKBOOK

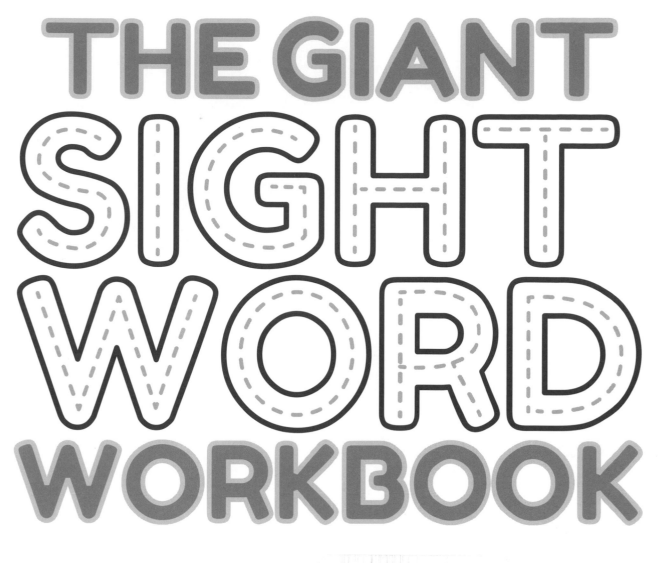

Diego Jourdan Pereira

THE GIANT SIGHT WORD WORKBOOK

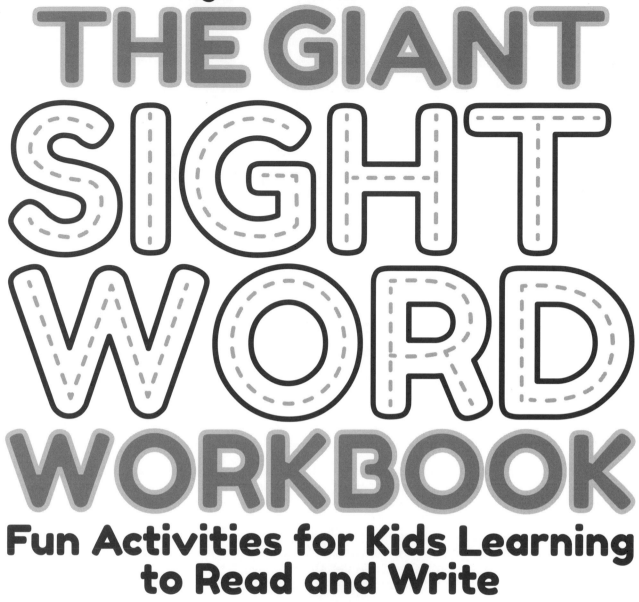

Fun Activities for Kids Learning to Read and Write

300 HIGH-FREQUENCY WORDS!

FOR YOUNG READERS

To my goddaughter, Carmen Elena.
May she grow into a fine young writer
someday!

Racehorse for Young Readers™ books may be purchased in bulk at special discounts for sales promotion, corporate gifts, fund-raising, or educational purposes. Special editions can also be created to specifications. For details, contact the Special Sales Department, Skyhorse Publishing, 307 West 36th Street, 11th Floor, New York, NY 10018 or info@skyhorsepublishing.com.

Racehorse for Young Readers™ is a pending trademark of Skyhorse Publishing, Inc.®, a Delaware corporation.

Visit our website at www.skyhorsepublishing.com.

10 9 8 7 6 5 4 3 2 1

Library of Congress Cataloging-in-Publication Data is available on file.

Cover and interior design by Diego Jourdan Pereira

Mechanical design by Kai Texel

Dot to Dot font designed by A New Machine at MyFonts.com. Used under license.

Fredoka One and Fredoka dingbats open fonts designed by Milena Brandao at FontSquirrel.com.

ISBN: 978-1-63158-673-6

Printed in China

A B C D E F G H I J K L M N O P Q R S T U V W X Y Z

🧸 CAN YOU WRITE THE LETTERS BY YOURSELF?

WRITE AND LEARN THE SIGHT WORDS.

am am am am am

am

are are are are are

are

and and and and

and

A B C D E F G H I J K L M N O P Q R S T U V W X Y Z

🦉 **It may be small but works very hard. What is it?**

ant ant ant

ant

ask ask ask

ask

🦉 **One a day keeps the doctor away. What is it?**

apple apple

apple

3

again again

again

aunt aunt

⭐ **Draw a portrait of your favorite aunt.**

aunt

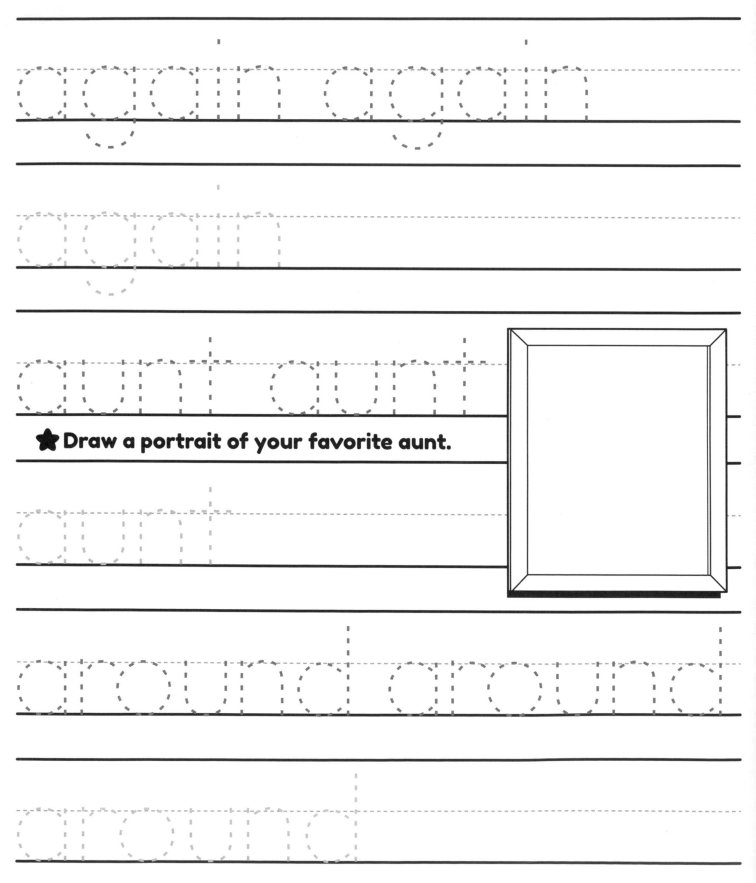

around around

around

above above

above

always always

always

answer answer

answer

★ TRACE, WRITE, AND COLOR!

Last April the

little apple

seed grew into

a tall

apple

tree

CAN YOU WRITE THE LETTERS BY YOURSELF?

🦉 **WRITE AND LEARN THE SIGHT WORDS.**

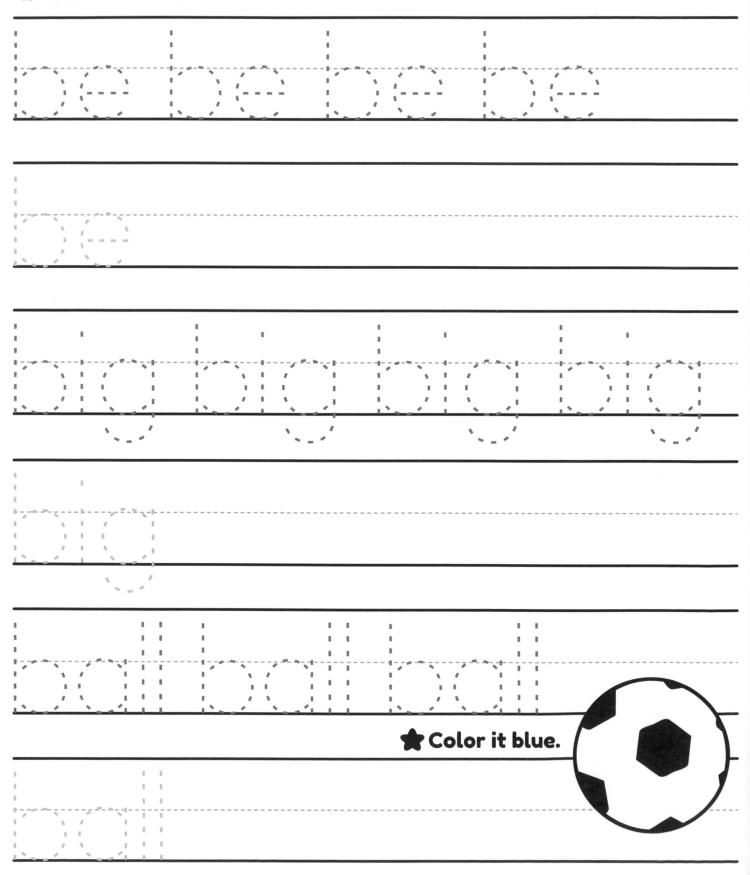

be be be be

be

big big big big

big

ball ball ball

⭐ **Color it blue.**

ball

bee bee bee

⭐ **Trace the bee's path to the flower.**

bee

blue blue blue

blue

bird bird bird

bird

back back

back

⭐ **Trace the dots to finish the drawing.**

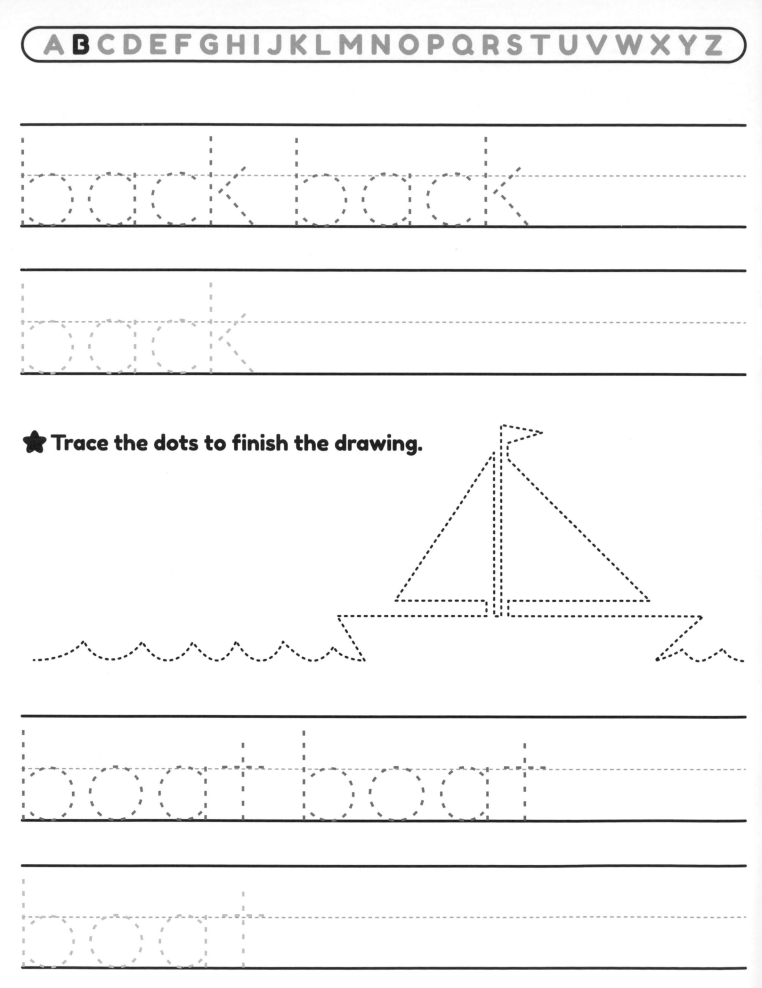

boat boat

boat

below below

below

both both

both

begin begin

begin

⭐ **TRACE, WRITE, AND COLOR!**

Both birds

love to fly

above

the big

blue

sea

CAN YOU WRITE THE LETTERS BY YOURSELF?

ABCDEFGHIJKLMNOPQRSTUVWXYZ

🦉 WRITE AND LEARN THE SIGHT WORDS.

can can can can

can

cat cat cat

cat

⭐ Draw the cat in three easy steps.

car car car

car

cow cow cow

cow

come come

come

cake cake cake

cake

color color color

🦉 **How many colors do you know?**

color

city city city

city

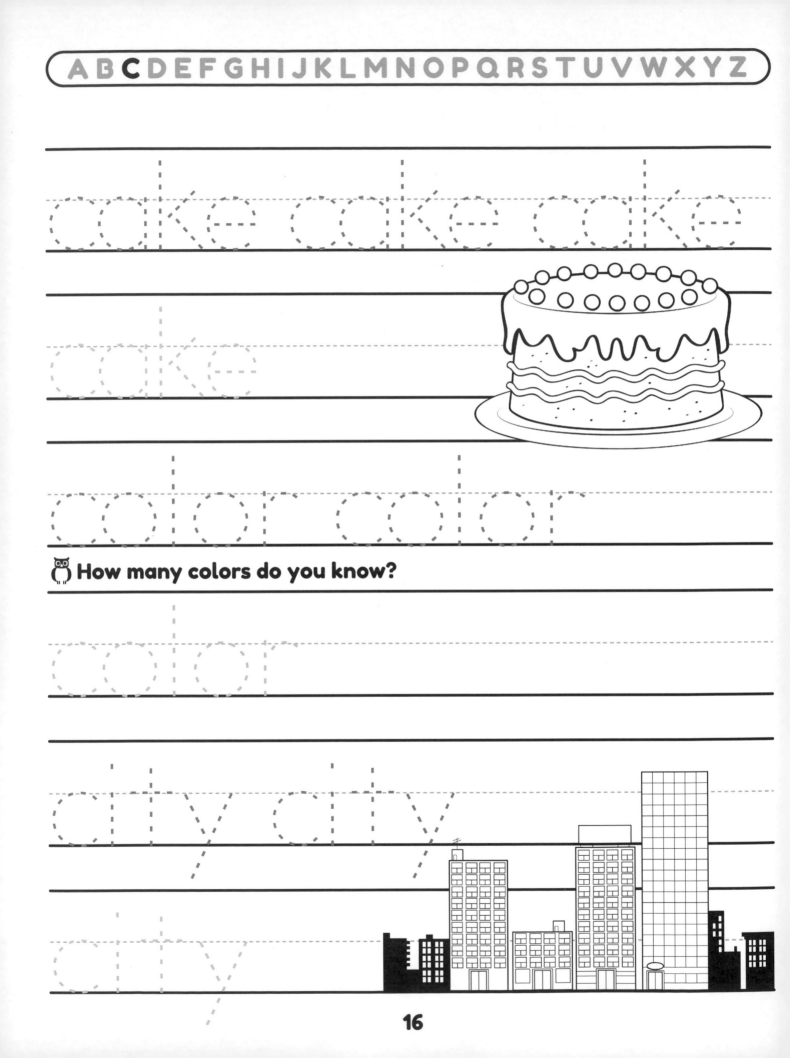

16

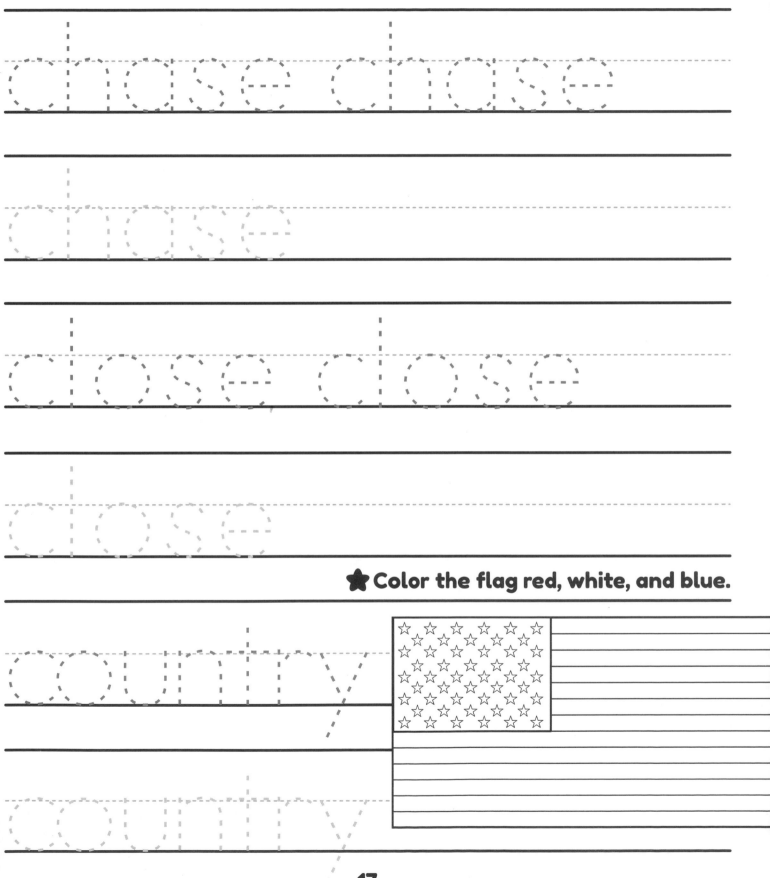

chase chase

chase

close close

close

★ Color the flag red, white, and blue.

country

country

⭐ TRACE, WRITE, AND COLOR!

Most city cats

love to chase

mice but these

two

are

close friends

A B C **D** E F G H I J K L M N O P Q R S T U V W X Y Z

CAN YOU WRITE THE LETTERS BY YOURSELF?

D D D D D D D

D D D D D D D

d d d d d d d

d d d d d d d

19

🦉 WRITE AND LEARN THE SIGHT WORDS.

do do do do do

do

does does

does

day day day

day

A B C **D** E F G H I J K L M N O P Q R S T U V W X Y Z

🦉 It's our best friend. Color it.

dog dog
dog
duck duck
duck

⭐ Which duck is different from the others?

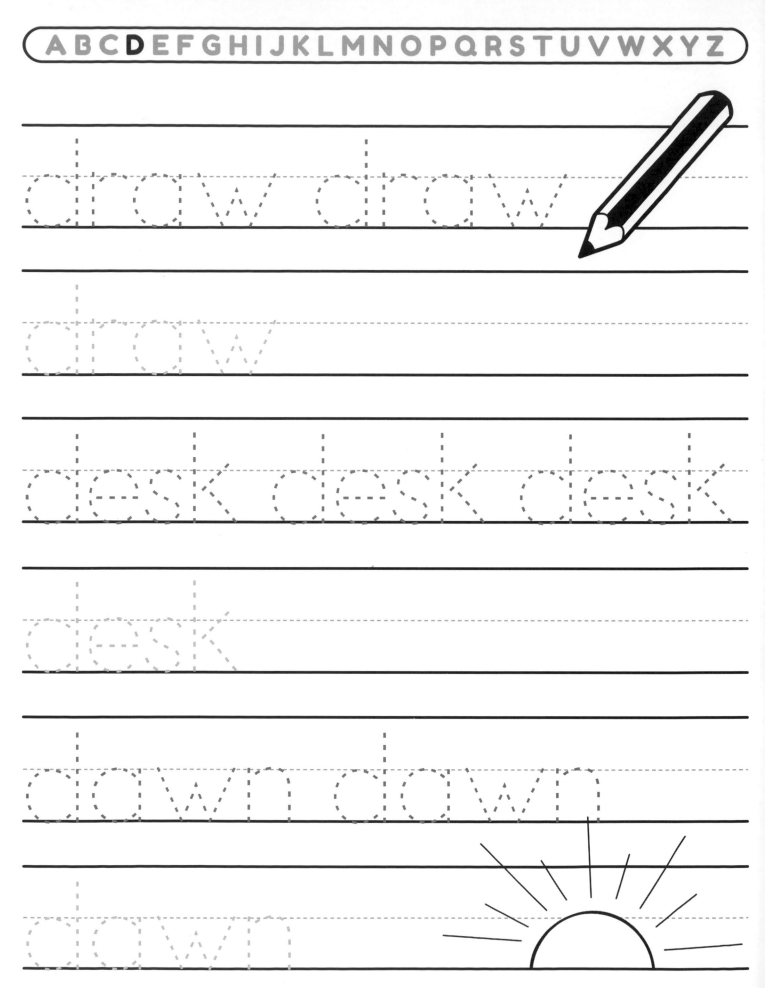

draw draw

draw

desk desk desk

desk

down down

down

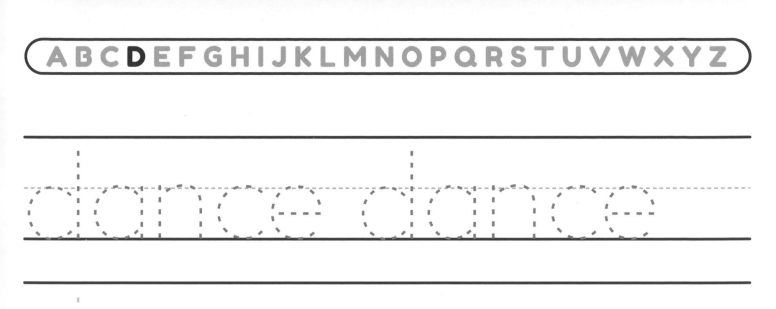

dance dance

dance

doctor doctor

doctor

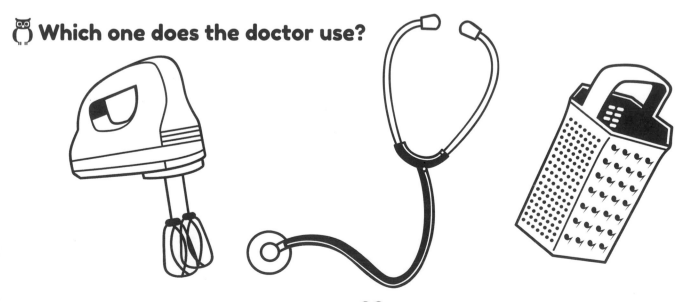

Which one does the doctor use?

⭐ **TRACE, WRITE, AND COLOR!**

Digby the dog

likes to play

in the park

all day

⭐ **Color Digby the dog.**

long.

24

A B C D **E** F G H I J K L M N O P Q R S T U V W X Y Z

CAN YOU WRITE THE LETTERS BY YOURSELF?

🦉 WRITE AND LEARN THE SIGHT WORDS.

ear ear ear

ear

eat eat

⭐ Color the food that's good for you.

eat

end end end

end

egg egg egg

egg

⭐ Trace and color the eggs.

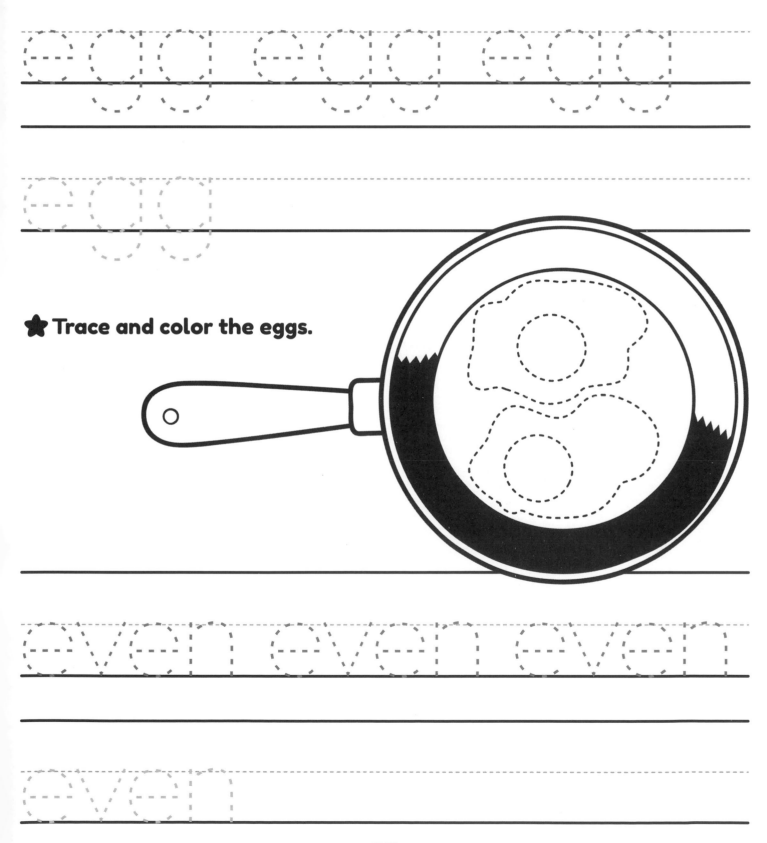

even even even

even

each each

each

earth earth

earth

🦉 **Do you know which one is the planet we live on? Color it.**

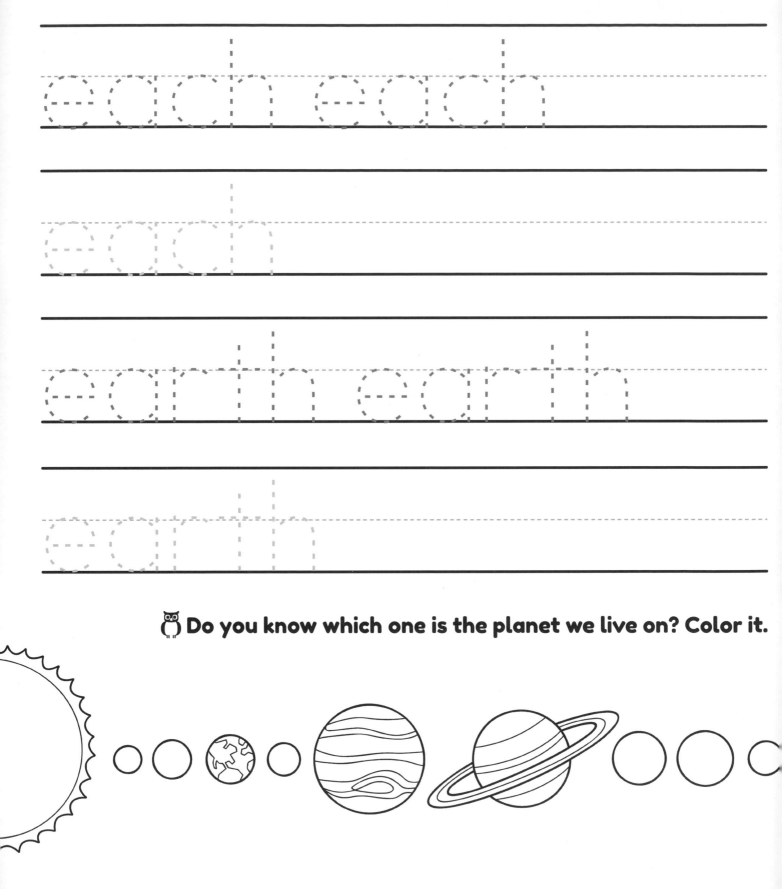

early early

early

every every

every

elephant

elephant

⭐ **TRACE, WRITE, AND COLOR!**

Elle

the elephant

eats tall grass

every evening

30

CAN YOU WRITE THE LETTERS BY YOURSELF?

🦉 **WRITE AND LEARN THE SIGHT WORDS.**

for for for for for

for

fly fly fly fly fly

fly

⭐ **Color the bird.**

few few few few

few

32

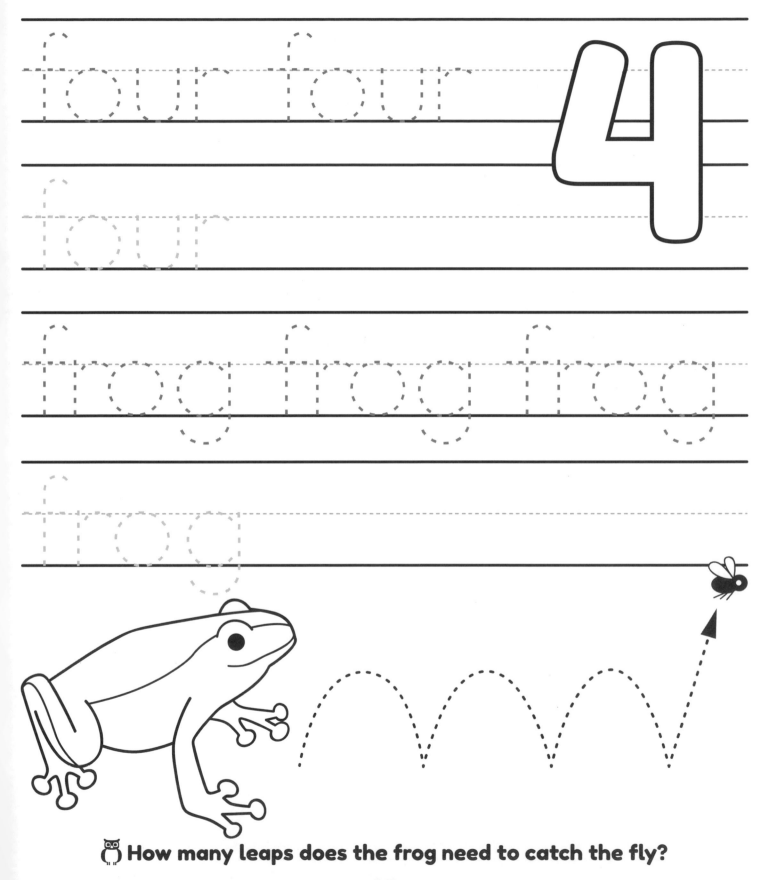

four four four

four

frog frog frog frog

frog

How many leaps does the frog need to catch the fly?

face face face

face

⭐ **Draw a happy face, a sad face, and a mad face.**

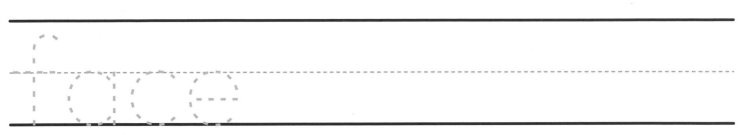

fork fork

🦉 **What do we use a fork for?**

fork

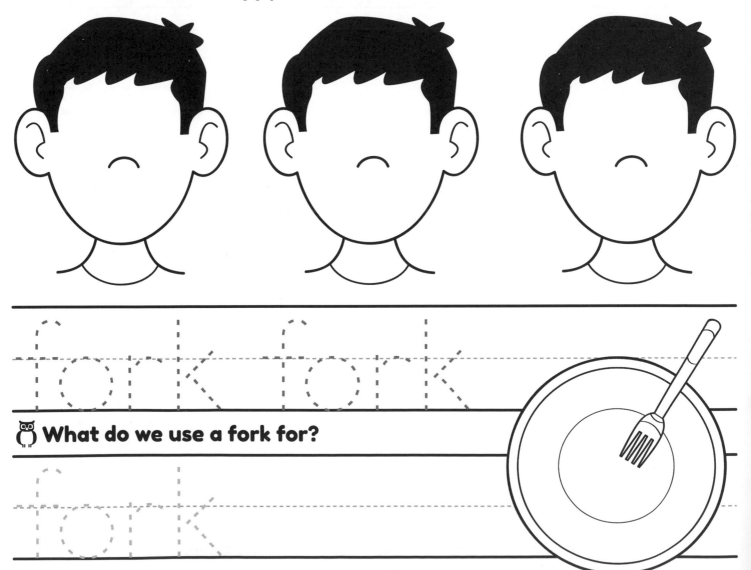

fruit fruit fruit

fruit

⭐ **Color the fruit below.**

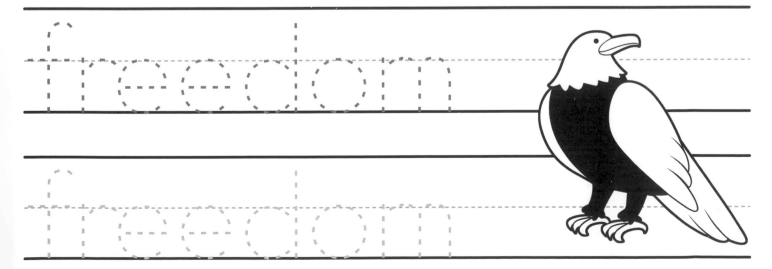

freedom

freedom

⭐ TRACE, WRITE, AND COLOR!

Frogs find
flies tasty
but if he eats
them all
he won't
like it

ABCDEF**G**HIJKLMNOPQRSTUVWXYZ

CAN YOU WRITE THE LETTERS BY YOURSELF?

G G G G G G

G G G G G G

a a a a a a a

a a a a a a a

37

🦉 WRITE AND LEARN THE SIGHT WORDS.

ABCDEF**G**HIJKLMNOPQRSTUVWXYZ

gift gift gift

gift

green green green

green

⭐ **Connect the dots and color it green.**

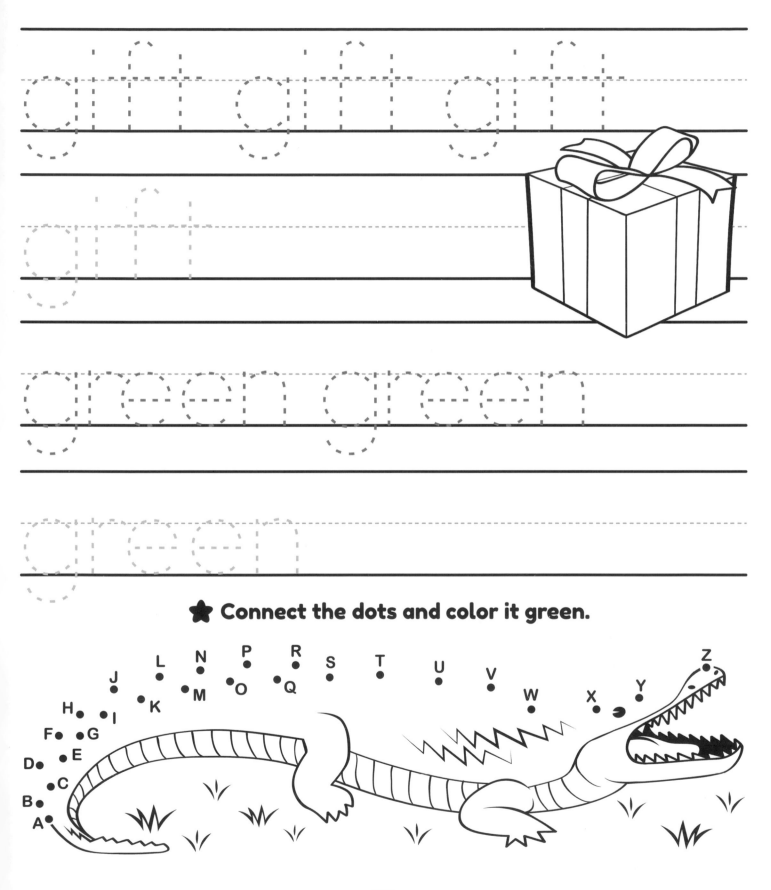

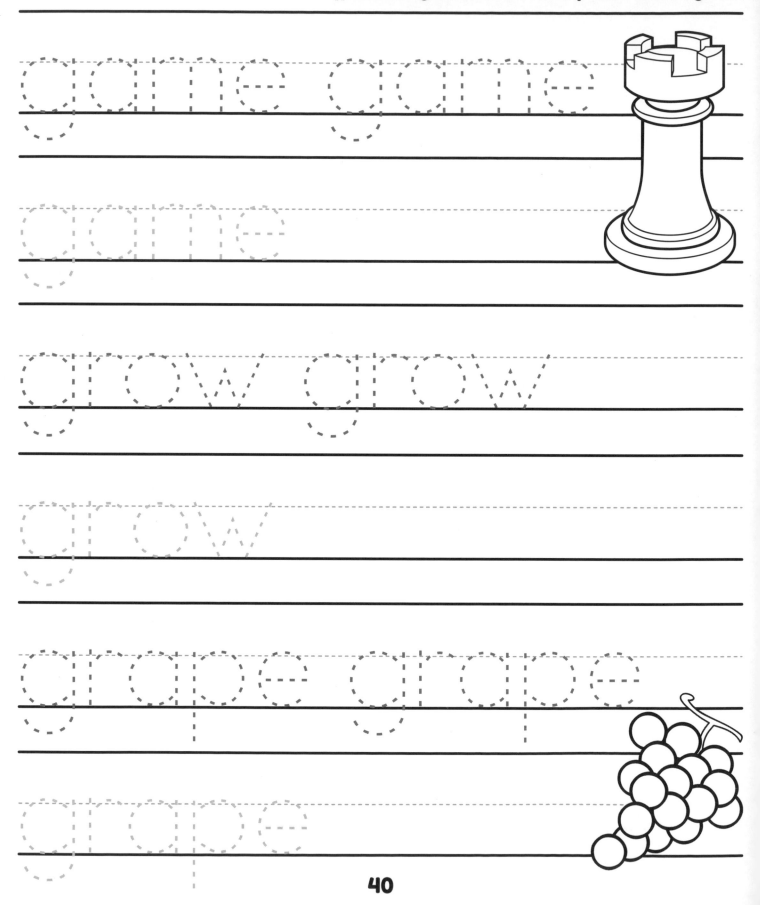

A B C D E F **G** H I J K L M N O P Q R S T U V W X Y Z

What game does this piece belong to?

game game

game

grow grow

grow

grape grape

grape

40

grass grass

grass

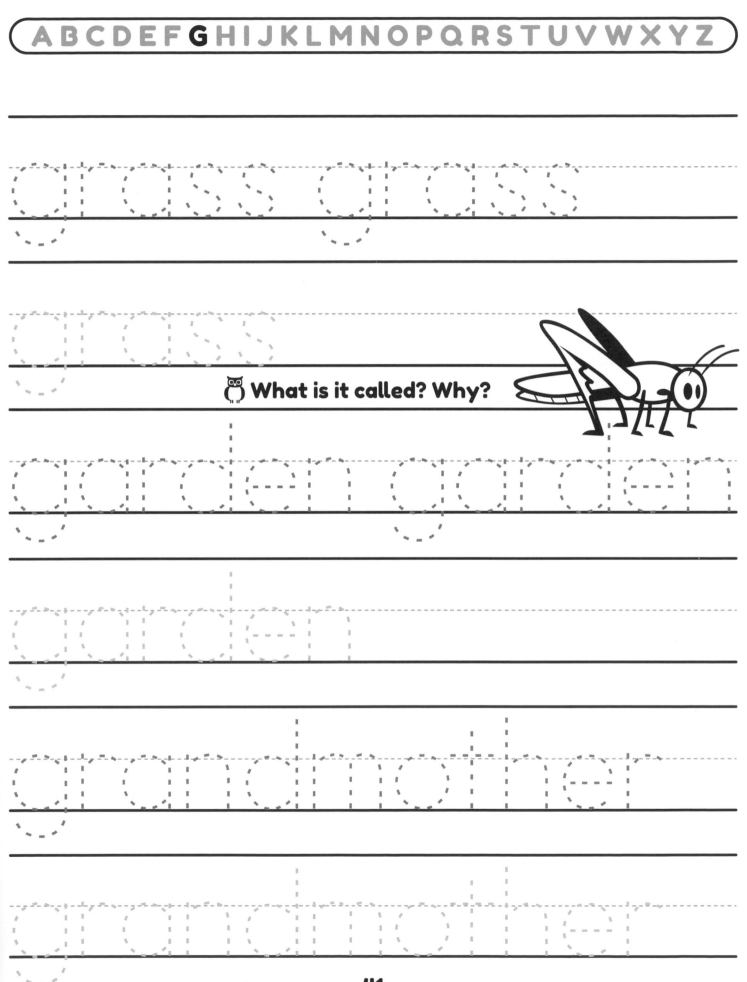

🦉 What is it called? Why?

garden garden

garden

grandmother

grandmother

⭐ TRACE, WRITE, AND COLOR!

Grandma has

a lovely green

cabbage patch

in her

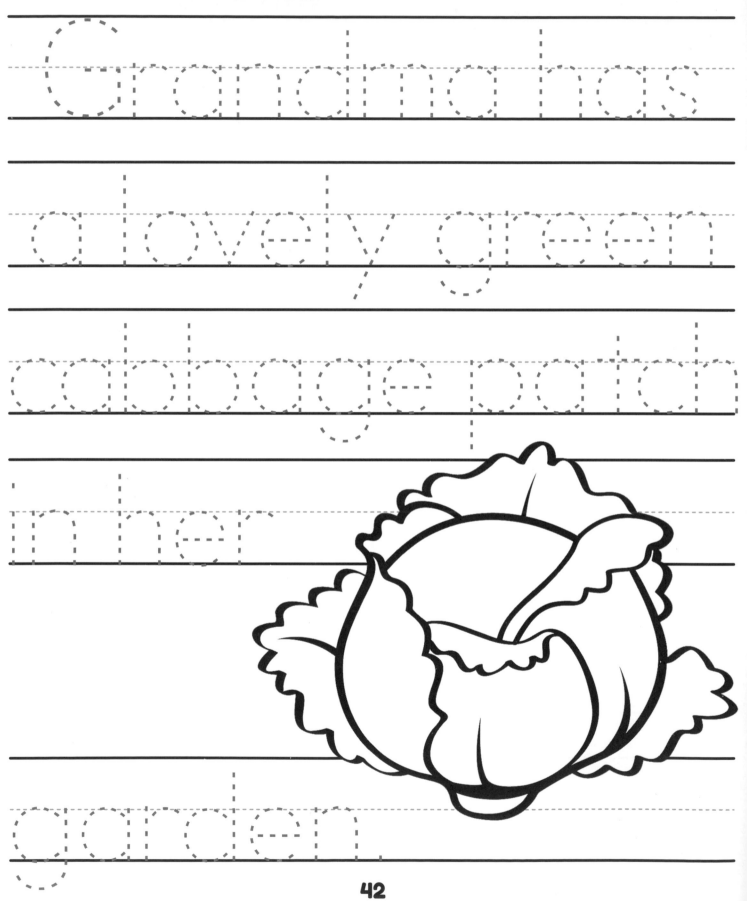

garden

42

CAN YOU WRITE THE LETTERS BY YOURSELF?

43

🦉 WRITE AND LEARN THE SIGHT WORDS.

he he he he he

he

hen hen hen

hen

how how how

how

hot hot hot hot hot

hot

⭐ Color only the hot stuff.

have have have

have

hair hair hair hair

hair

⭐ Give her different haircuts.

home home

home

happy happy

happy

horse horse

horse

honey honey

honey

HONEY

⭐ TRACE, WRITE, AND COLOR!

If I was a horse

I would run

and I would

prance

happily

all around

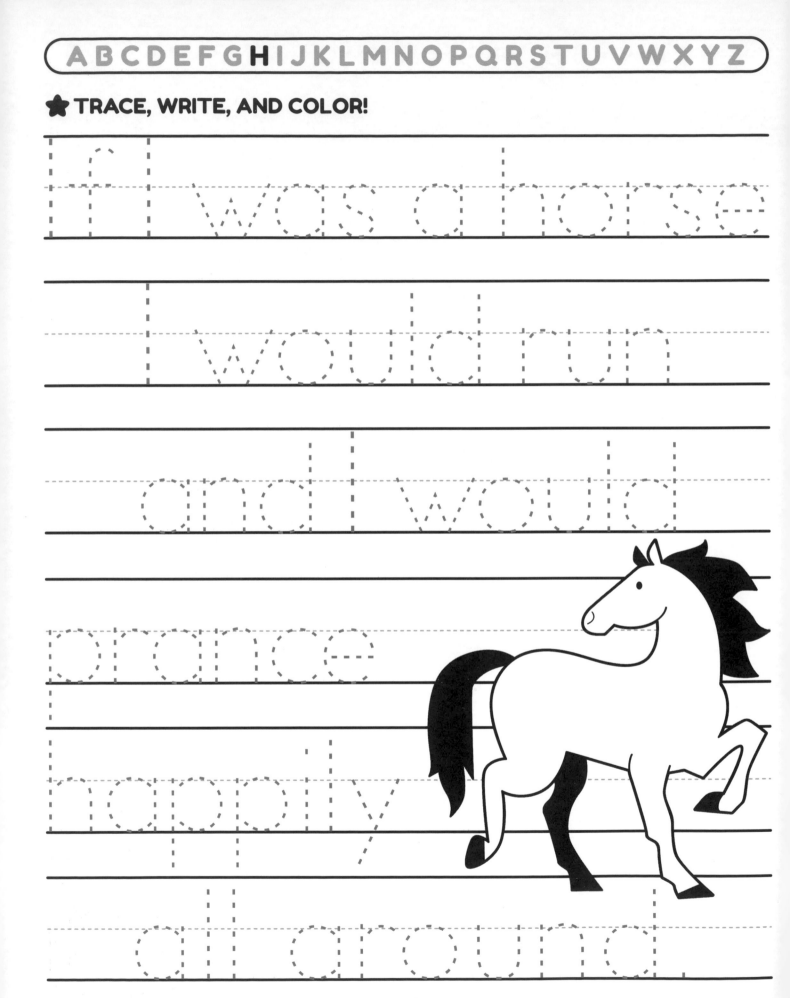

ABCDEFGHIJKLMNOPQRSTUVWXYZ

CAN YOU WRITE THE LETTERS BY YOURSELF?

ABCDEFGH**I**JKLMNOPQRSTUVWXYZ

🦉 WRITE AND LEARN THE SIGHT WORDS.

is is is is is is is

is

in in in in in in in

in

50

if if if if if if if if

if

ice ice ice ice

🦉 What is ice made of?

ice

idea idea idea idea

idea

iron iron iron

🦉 **What are horseshoes made of?**

iron

invent invent

invent

⭐ **Invent your own robots using the parts below.**

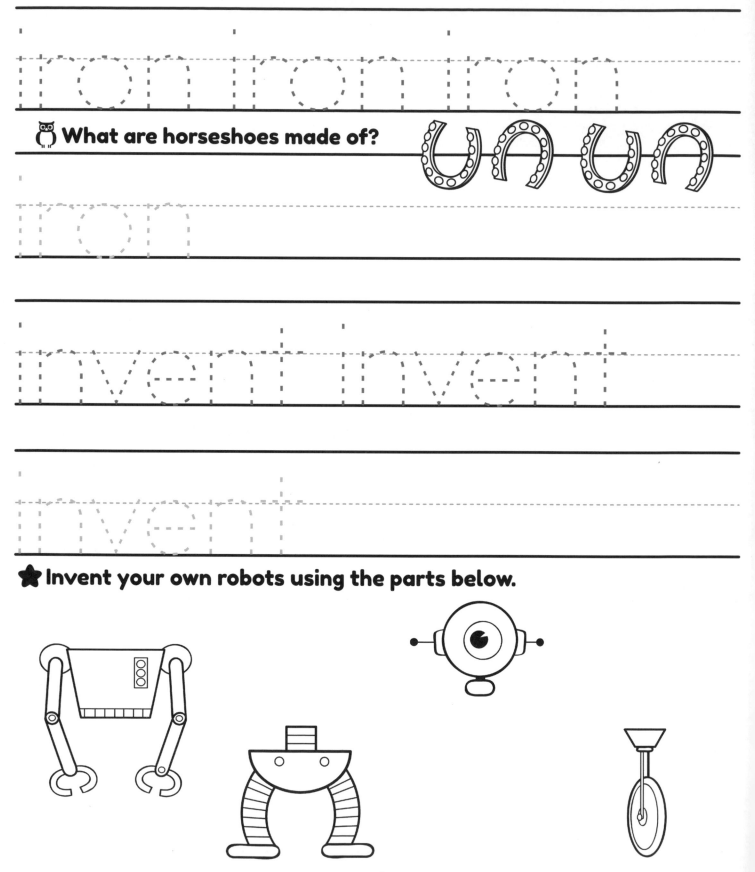

inside inside

🦉 **Where does she live?**

inside

island island

island

important

important

ABCDEFGH**I**JKLMNOPQRSTUVWXYZ

⭐ **TRACE, WRITE, AND COLOR!**

All Mr. Penguin

wanted was

ice cream

but all he

found

was fish

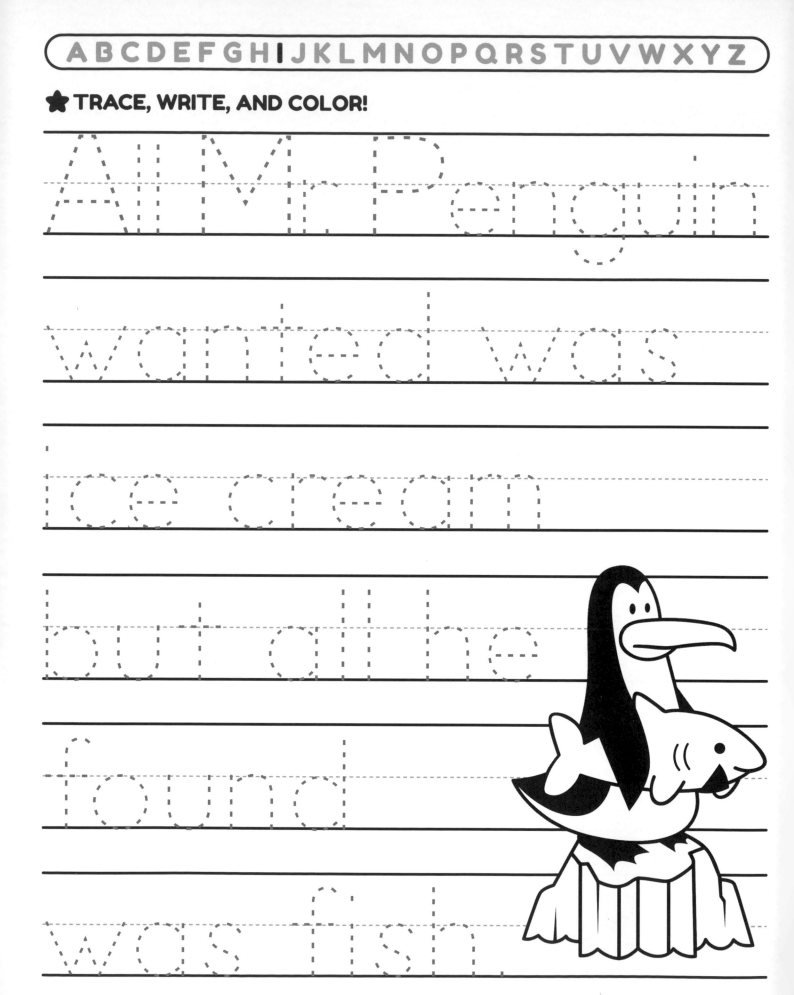

54

ABCDEFGHIJKLMNOPQRSTUVWXYZ

🧸 CAN YOU WRITE THE LETTERS BY YOURSELF?

55

WRITE AND LEARN THE SIGHT WORDS.

job job job job job

job

joy joy joy joy joy

joy

⭐ Draw as much candy as you can inside.

jar jar jar

jar

join join join

join

⭐ **Draw the missing paper doll to join them.**

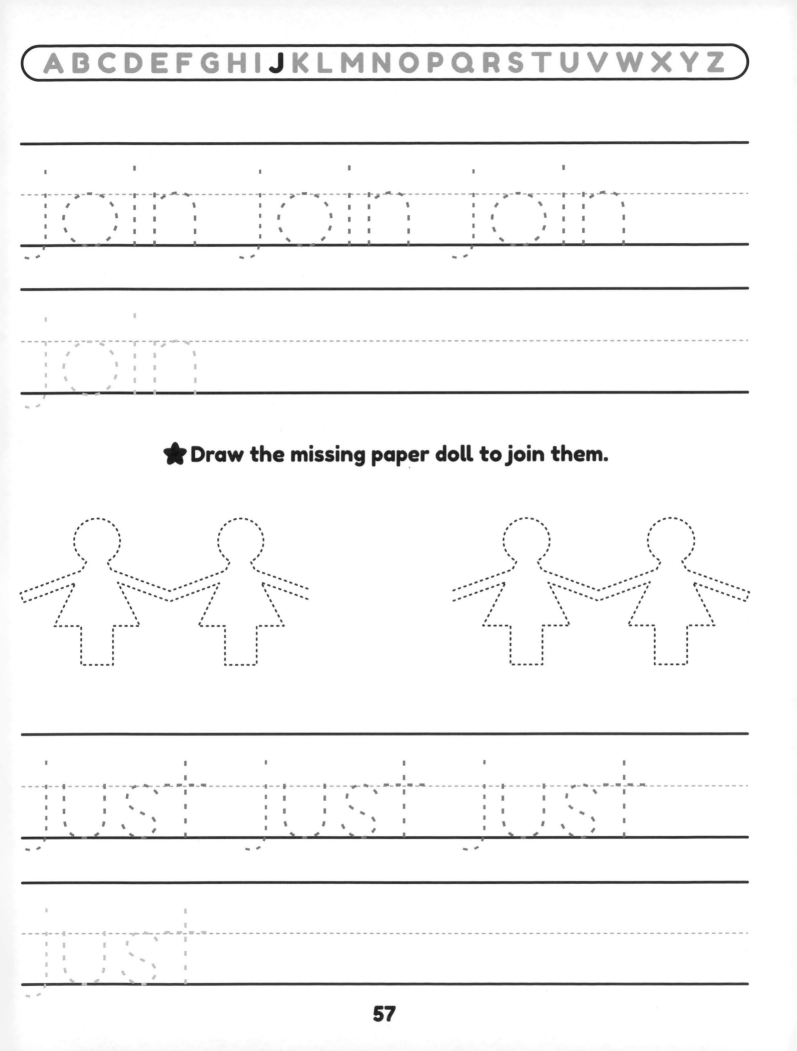

just just just

just

jump jump

jump

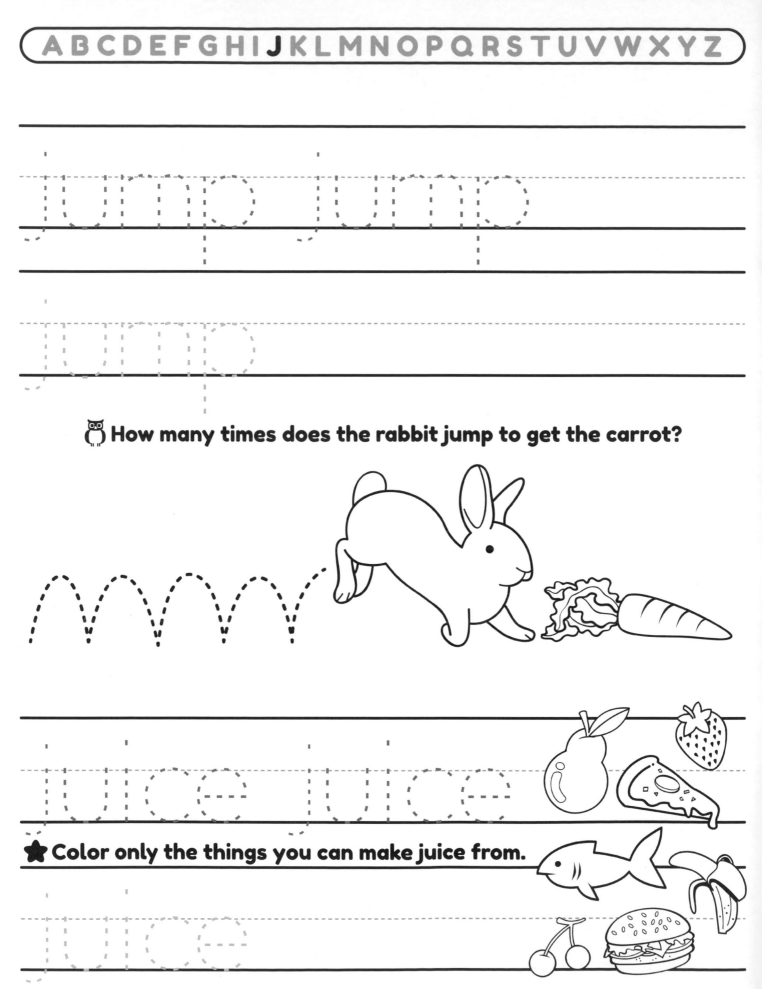

🦉 **How many times does the rabbit jump to get the carrot?**

juice juice

⭐ **Color only the things you can make juice from.**

juice

jelly jelly jelly

jelly

jungle jungle

jungle

🦉 **Where does the monkey live?**

jacket jacket

jacket

A B C D E F G H I **J** K L M N O P Q R S T U V W X Y Z

⭐ TRACE, WRITE, AND COLOR!

Jelly beans

jumping

all around

Color and

count them

all with joy

60

CAN YOU WRITE THE LETTERS BY YOURSELF?

🦉 WRITE AND LEARN THE SIGHT WORDS.

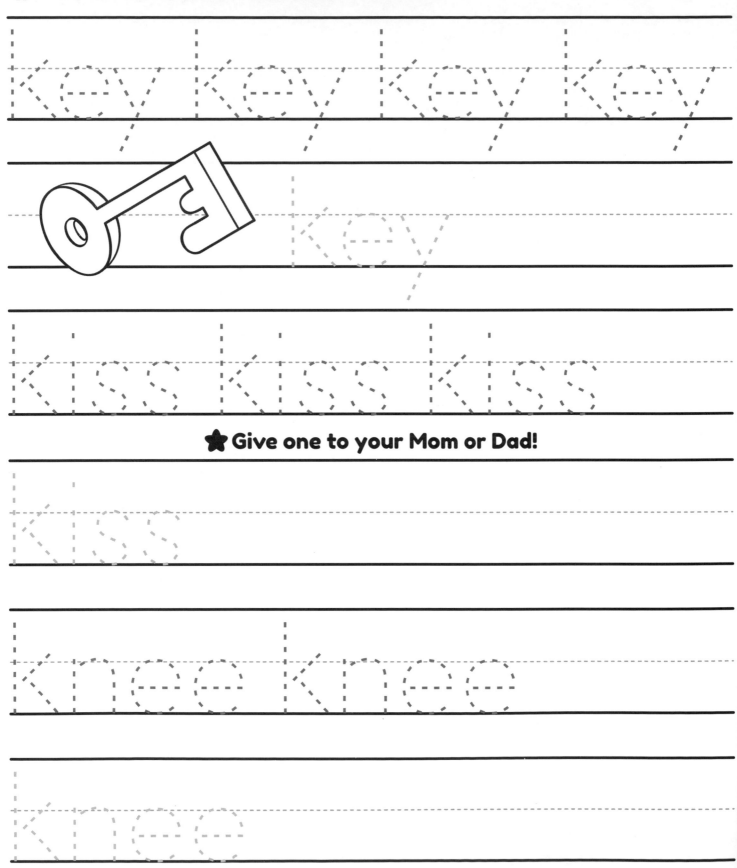

key key key key

key

kiss kiss kiss

⭐ Give one to your Mom or Dad!

kiss

knee knee

knee

kite kite kite

kite

⭐ Decorate and color the kite any way you like.

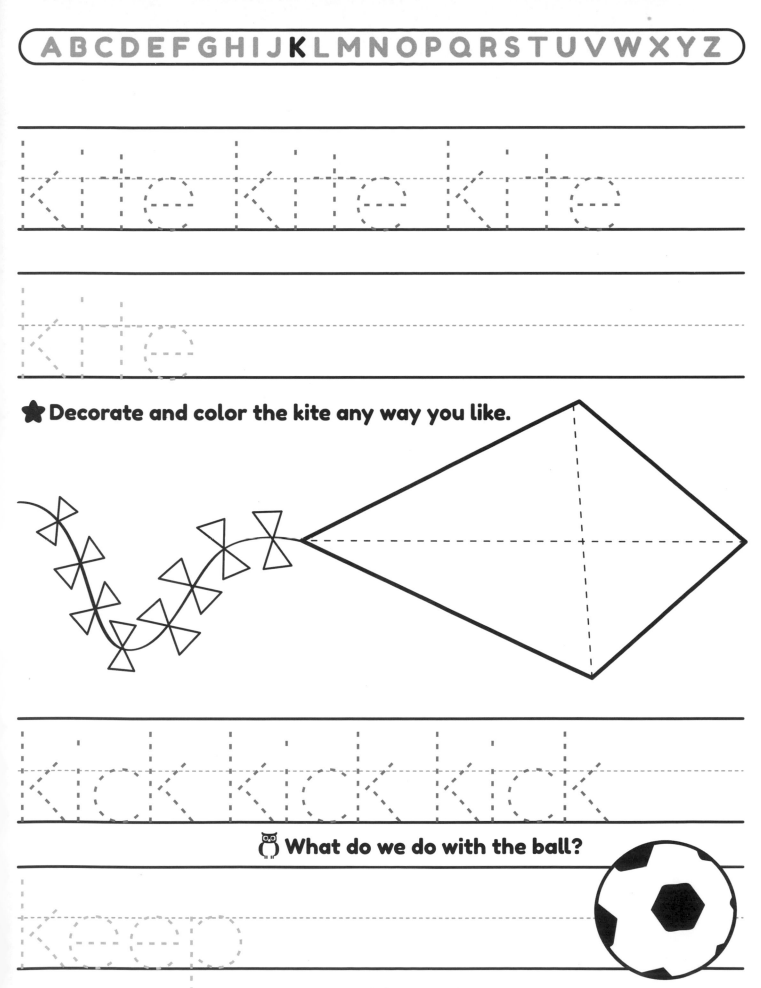

kick kick kick

🦉 What do we do with the ball?

keep

kind kind kind

kind

king king king

king

What would you do with the treasure?

keep keep

keep

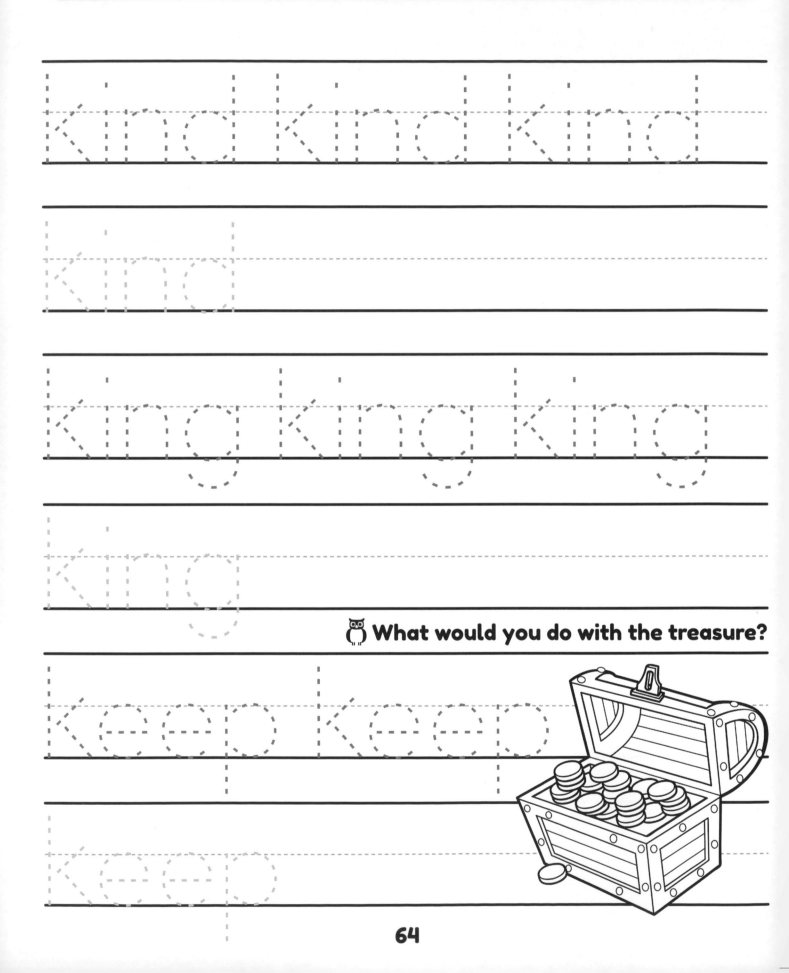

ABCDEFGHIJ**K**LMNOPQRSTUVWXYZ

kettle kettle

🦉 **What is a kettle for?**

kettle

kitchen kitchen

kitchen

🦉 **Where do we find all of these?**

⭐ **Can you draw another item below?**

65

⭐ **TRACE, WRITE, AND COLOR!**

The kind king

lost his mane.

Give him one

he can

keep.

A B C D E F G H I J K **L** M N O P Q R S T U V W X Y Z

CAN YOU WRITE THE LETTERS BY YOURSELF?

A B C D E F G H I J K **L** M N O P Q R S T U V W X Y Z

67

🦉 WRITE AND LEARN THE SIGHT WORDS.

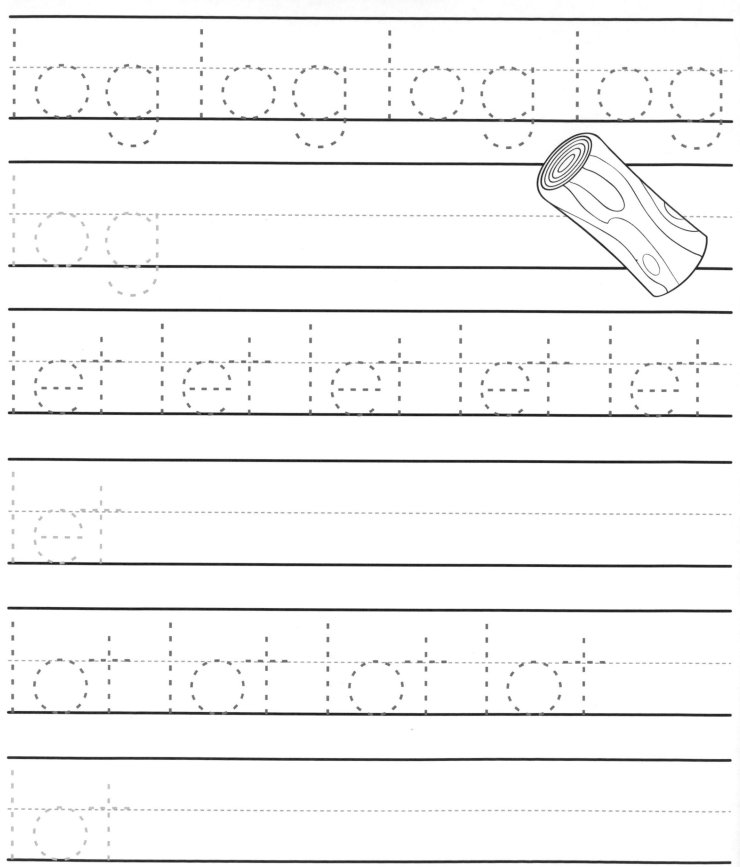

less less less

less

love love love

love

What does the heart stand for? How many can you count?

left left left

left

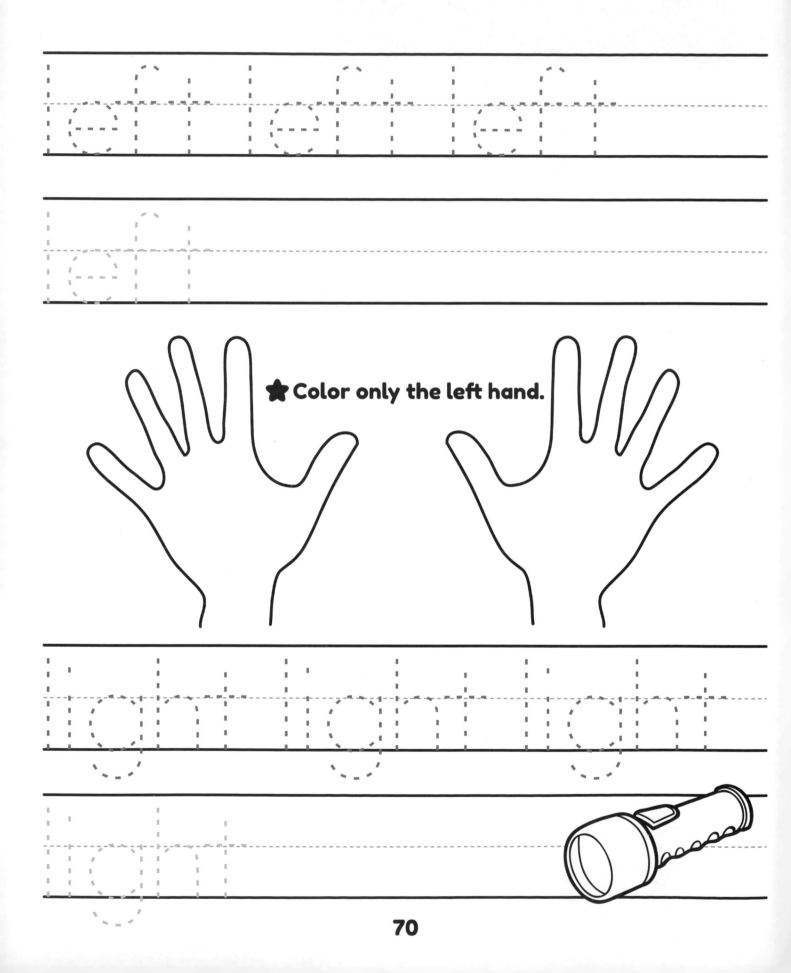

⭐ Color only the left hand.

light light light

light

look look look

look

🦉 **What are glasses for?**

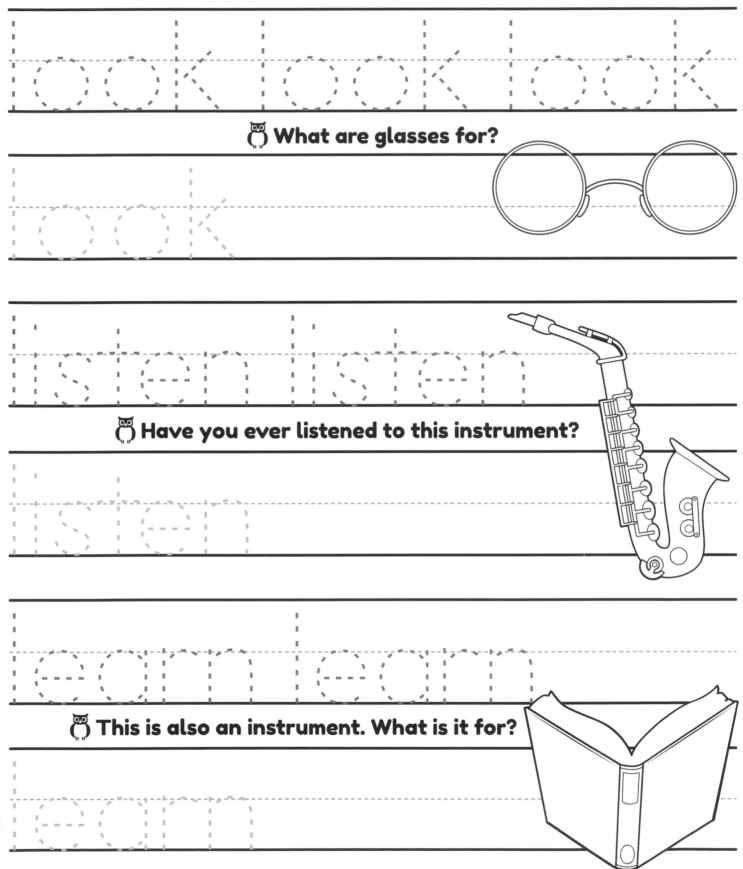

listen listen

🦉 **Have you ever listened to this instrument?**

listen

learn learn

🦉 **This is also an instrument. What is it for?**

learn

⭐ TRACE, WRITE, AND COLOR!

Louie the owl loves to stay up late while reading under the moonlight

🐾 CAN YOU WRITE THE LETTERS BY YOURSELF?

🦉 WRITE AND LEARN THE SIGHT WORDS.

me me me

⭐ Draw your own portrait.

me

my my my my my

my

mom mom mom

mom

map map map map

map

⭐ **What country is this?**
Fill each state with a different color.

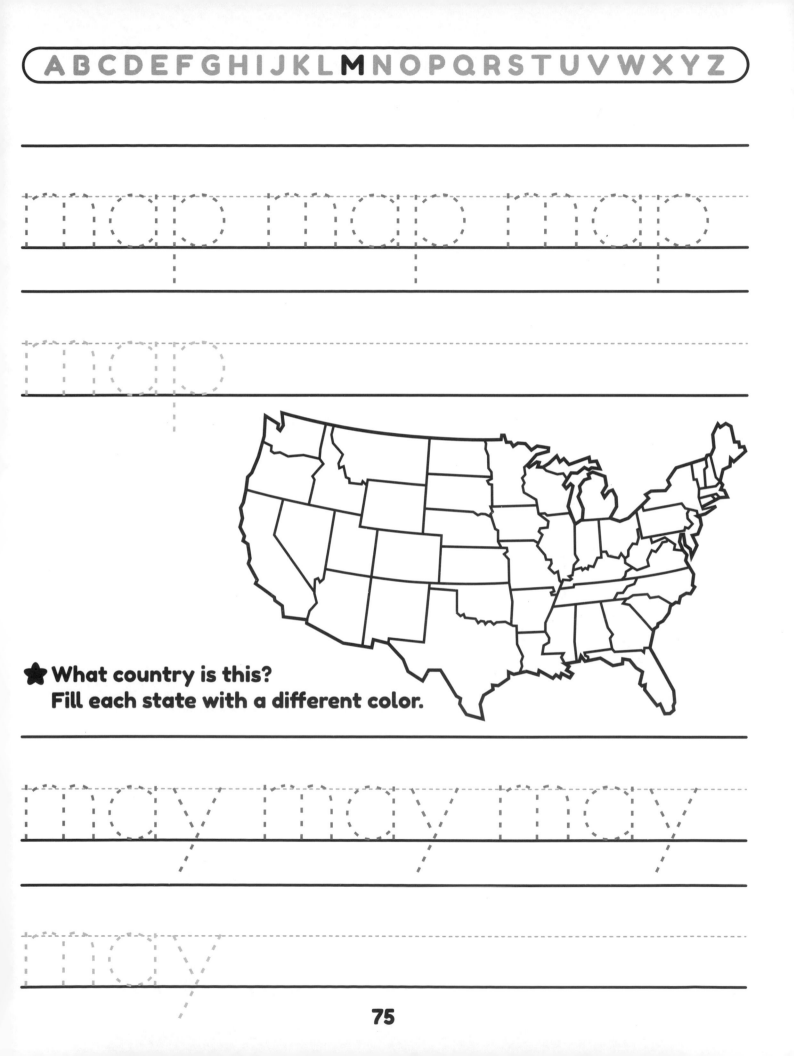

may may may

may

maze maze maze

maze

★ Help the mouse out of the maze to find the cheese.

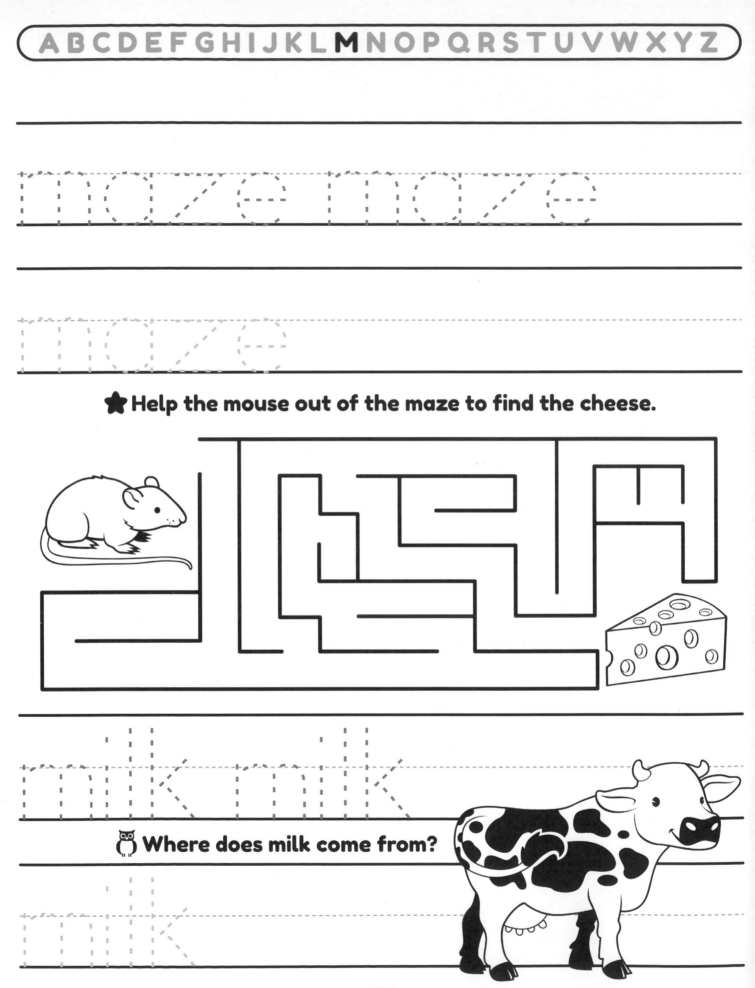

milk milk milk

🦉 Where does milk come from?

milk

ABCDEFGHIJKL**M**NOPQRSTUVWXYZ

meat meat

meat

🦉 **What are most sandwiches made with?**

mother

⭐ **Draw your mom's portrait.**

mother

77

⭐ **TRACE, WRITE, AND COLOR!**

My mother

likes to pour

milk into her

coffee

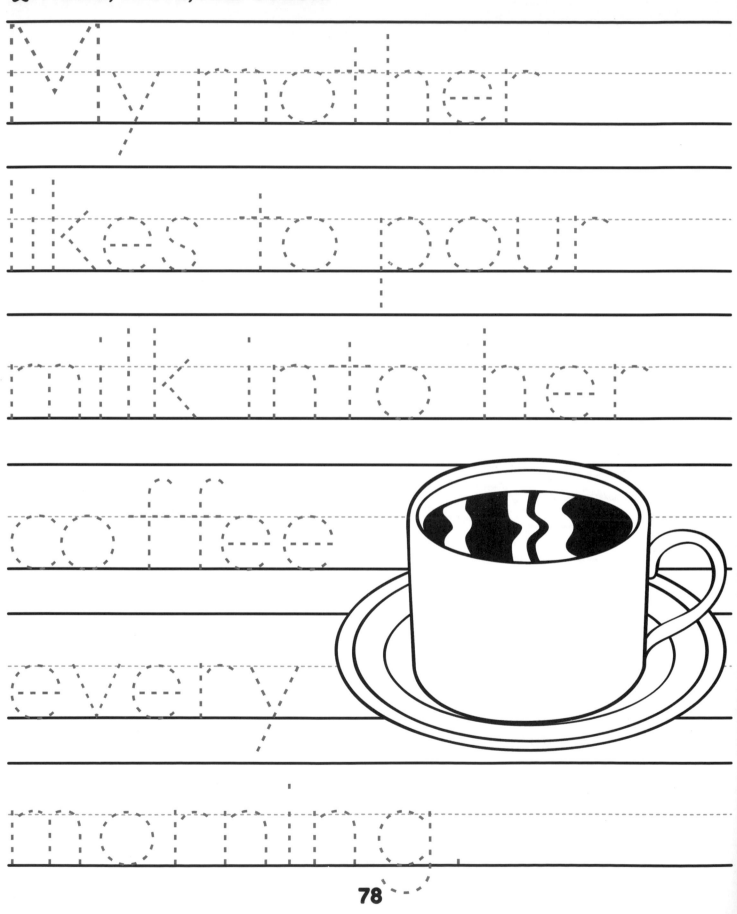

every

morning

CAN YOU WRITE THE LETTERS BY YOURSELF?

🦉 WRITE AND LEARN THE SIGHT WORDS.

no no no no no no no

no

⭐ Color the sign red.

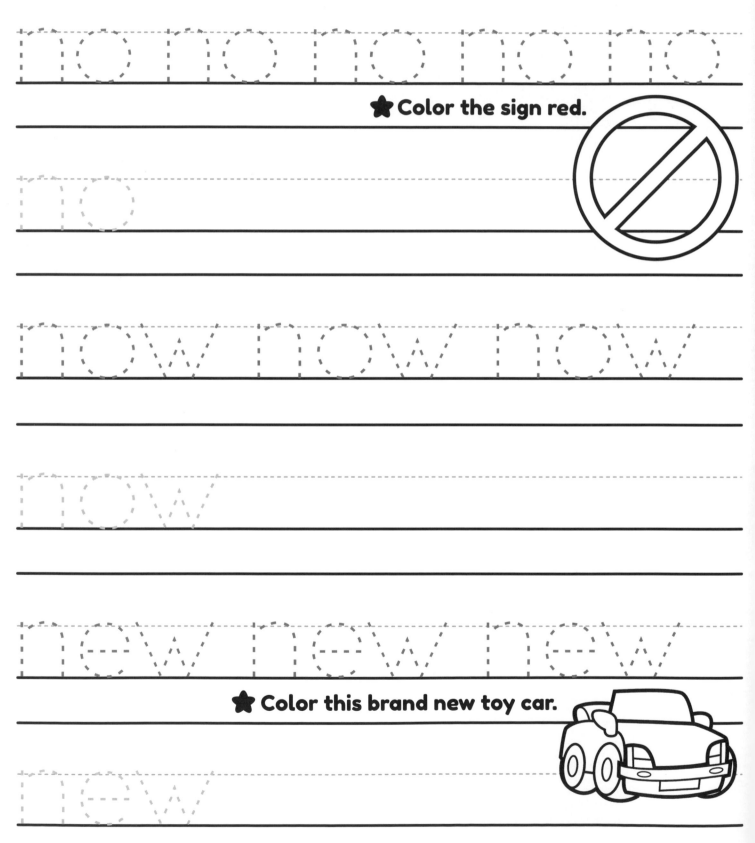

now now now

now

new new new

⭐ Color this brand new toy car.

new

name name name

name

⭐ **Can you write your first name below?**

⭐ **Can you write your last name below?**

nice nice nice

nice

nest nest nest

nest

⭐ Trace the line, to help her reach her nest.

near near near

near

need need

need

⭐ **If you need something, draw it here.**

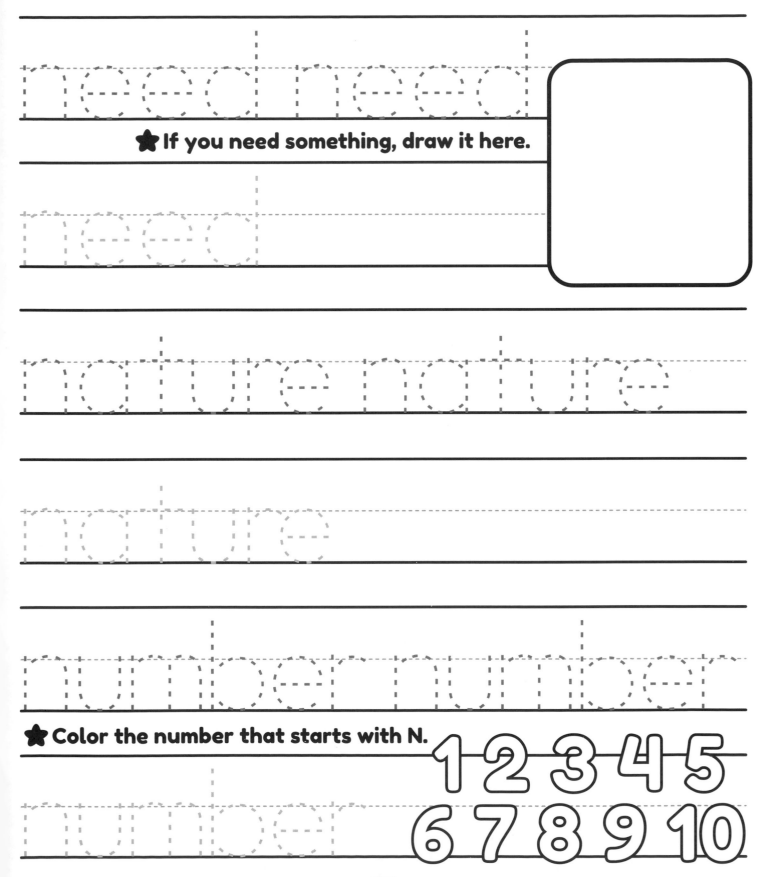

nature nature

nature

number number

⭐ **Color the number that starts with N.**

1 2 3 4 5
6 7 8 9 10

number

⭐ TRACE, WRITE, AND COLOR!

Nadia the

nesting doll

always keeps

her nine girls

near her

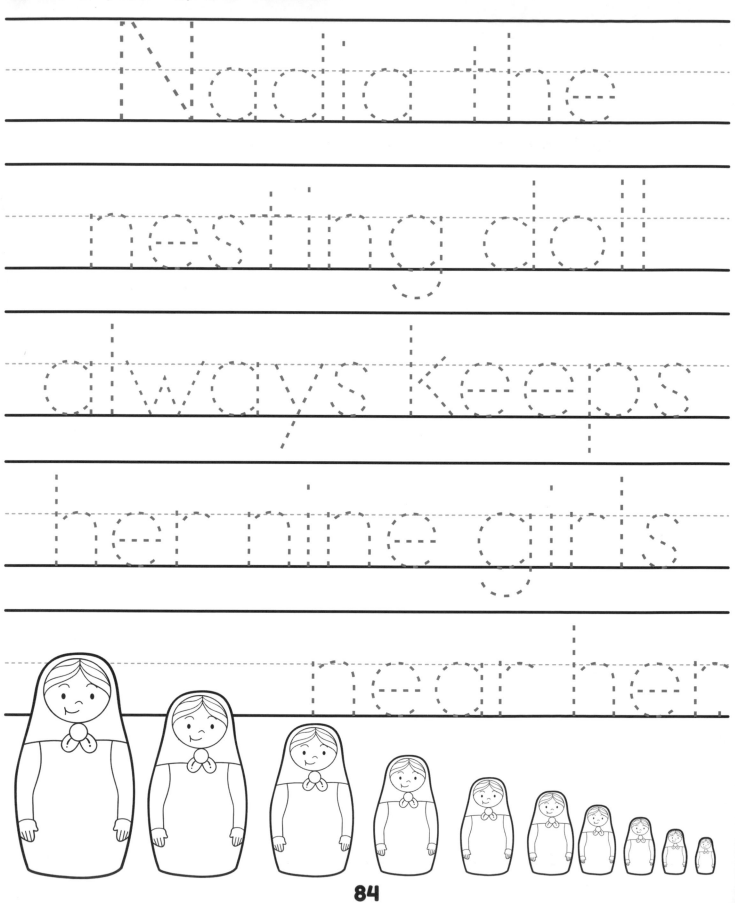

CAN YOU WRITE THE LETTERS BY YOURSELF?

A B C D E F G H I J K L M N **O** P Q R S T U V W X Y Z

🦉 WRITE AND LEARN THE SIGHT WORDS.

of of of of of of of of

of

THE UNITED STATES ☐ ← 🦉 **What is it missing?**
AMERICA

or or or or or or or or

or or or or or or or or

86

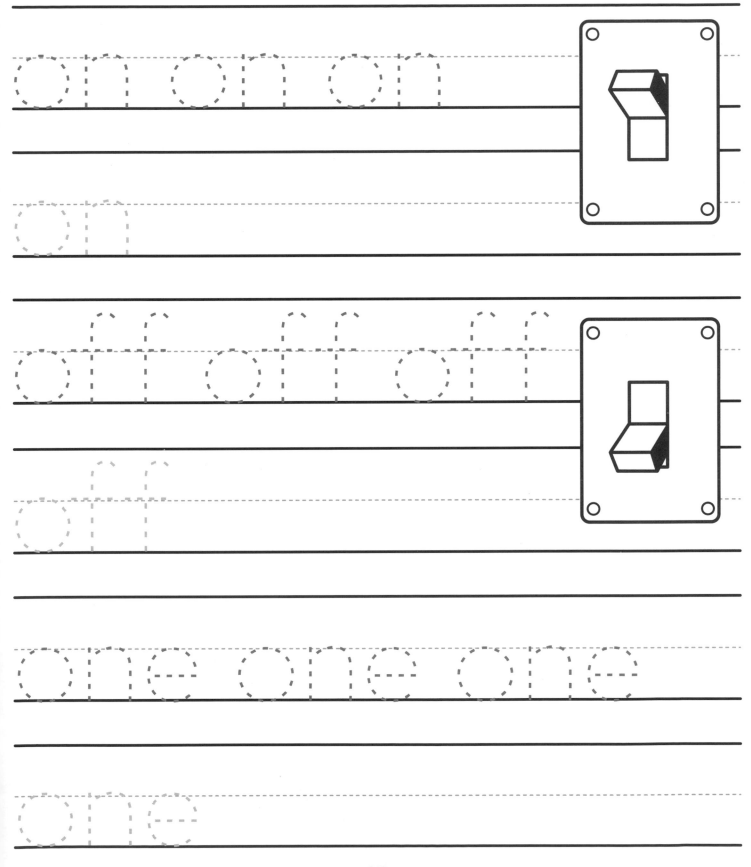

on on on

on

off off off

off

one one one

one

open open

open

owl owl owl

owl

How many owls are asleep?

once once

once

ocean ocean

ocean

They live in the ocean. What are they called?

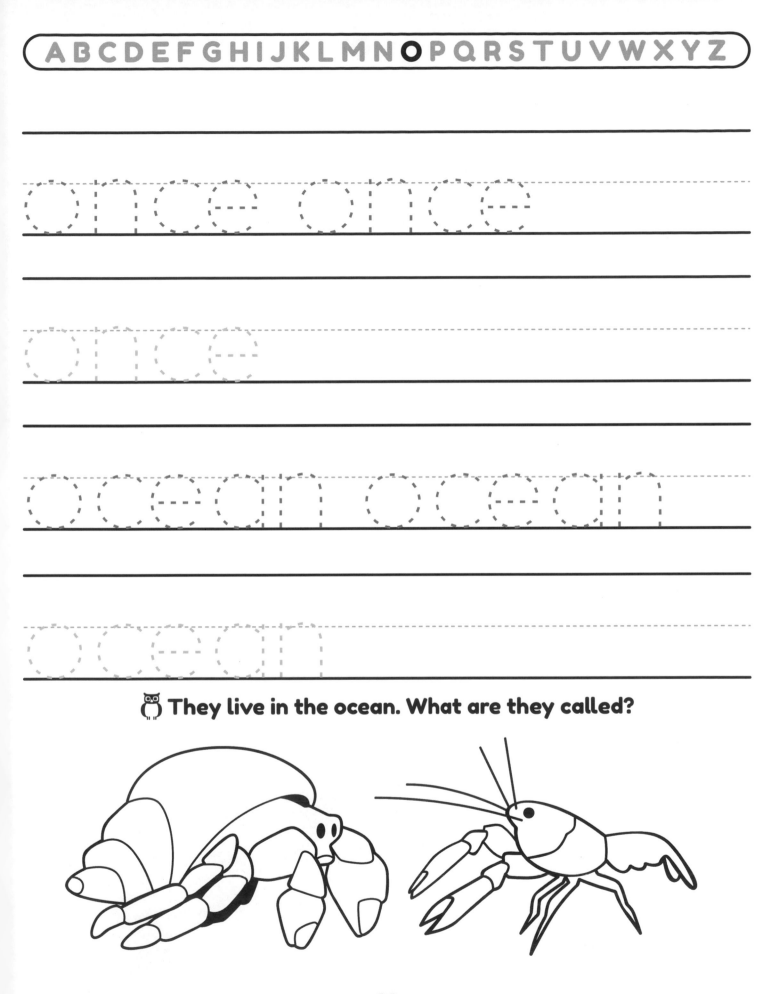

⭐ TRACE, WRITE, AND COLOR!

Omar the

orca was seen

swimming in the

open ocean

one day

A B C D E F G H I J K L M N O **P** Q R S T U V W X Y Z

CAN YOU WRITE THE LETTERS BY YOURSELF?

🦉 WRITE AND LEARN THE SIGHT WORDS.

pay pay pay

pay

🦉 What do we pay with?

⭐ Color the small coins red, and the big ones yellow.

pig pig pig pig

pig

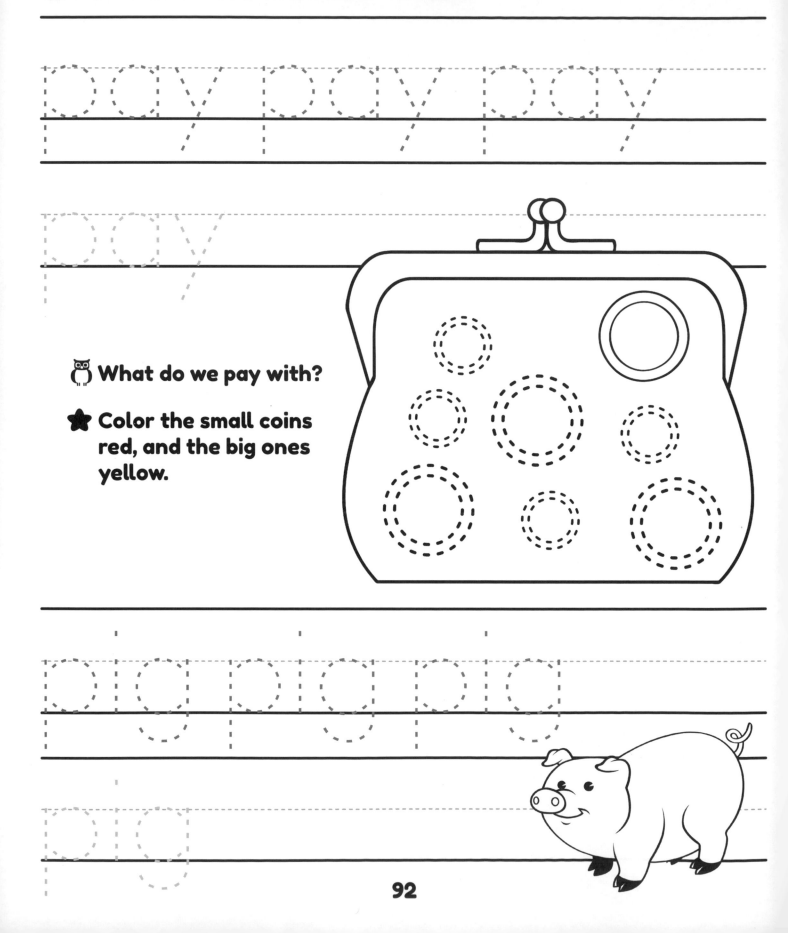

92

pair pair pair

pair

★ Color the cotton candy pink.

pink pink

pink

🦉 Which sports do we play with each of the balls below?

play play play

play

paint paint

paint

🦉 **What are brushes for?**

plane plane

plane

🦉 **Which shadow doesn't match the plane?**

ABCDEFGHIJKLMNO**P**QRSTUVWXYZ

pencil pencil

pencil

people people

people

🦉 **Where does this fruit come from?**

pineapple

pineapple

95

⭐ TRACE, WRITE, AND COLOR!

The pink pig

paints himself

brown with

mud from his

pigpen

ABCDEFGHIJKLMNOP**Q**RSTUVWXYZ

CAN YOU WRITE THE LETTERS BY YOURSELF?

🦉 **WRITE AND LEARN THE SIGHT WORDS.**

quiz quiz

quiz

quite quite

quite

quest quest

quest

98

quilt quilt

quilt

quiet quiet

quiet

quick quick

quick

A B C D E F G H I J K L M N O P **Q** R S T U V W X Y Z

quack quack

quack

🦉 **What noise does each animal make? Which one quacks?**

queen queen

queen

100

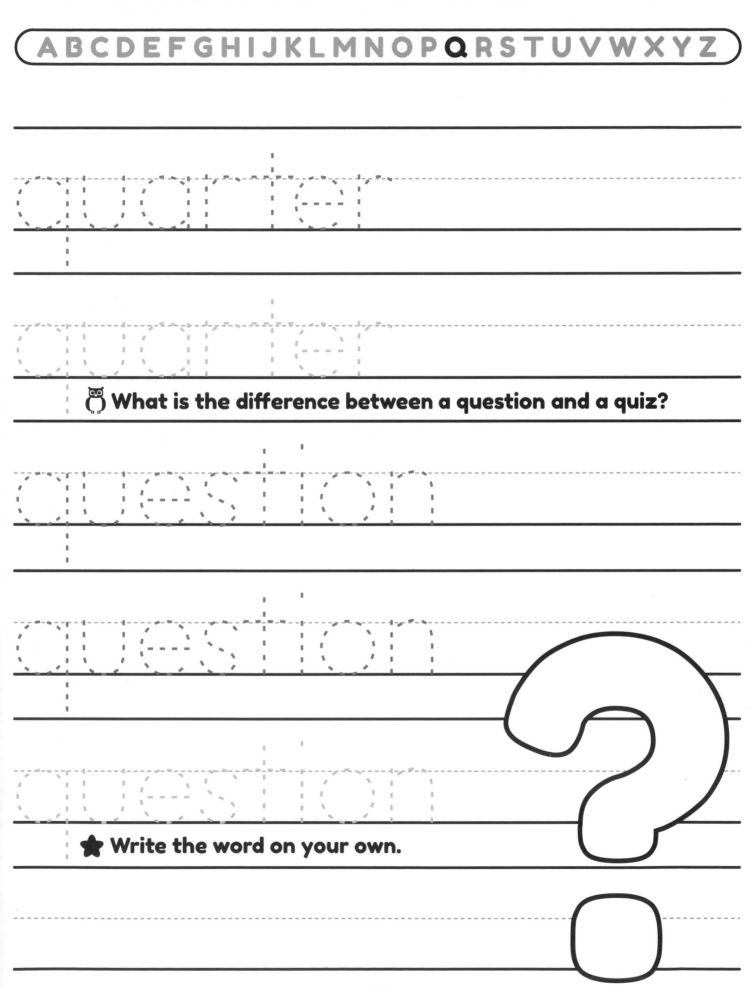

ABCDEFGHIJKLMNOP**Q**RSTUVWXYZ

quarter

quarter

🦉 **What is the difference between a question and a quiz?**

question

question

⭐ **Write the word on your own.**

101

⭐ TRACE, WRITE, AND COLOR!

Quiet little

rabbits

are known

for being

quite quick

on their feet

CAN YOU WRITE THE LETTERS BY YOURSELF?

WRITE AND LEARN THE SIGHT WORDS.

red red red red red

red

⭐ Color them red.

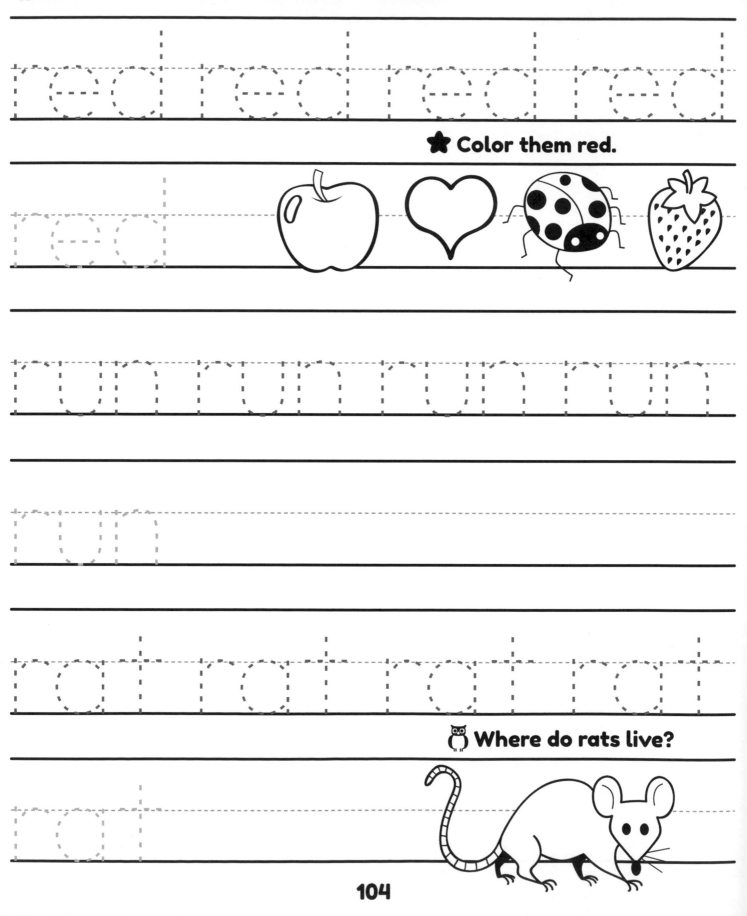

run run run run run

run

rat rat rat rat rat

🦉 Where do rats live?

rat

ABCDEFGHIJKLMNOPQ**R**STUVWXYZ

rain rain rain

🦉 **What is rain made of?**

rain

real real real

real

ring ring

ring

105

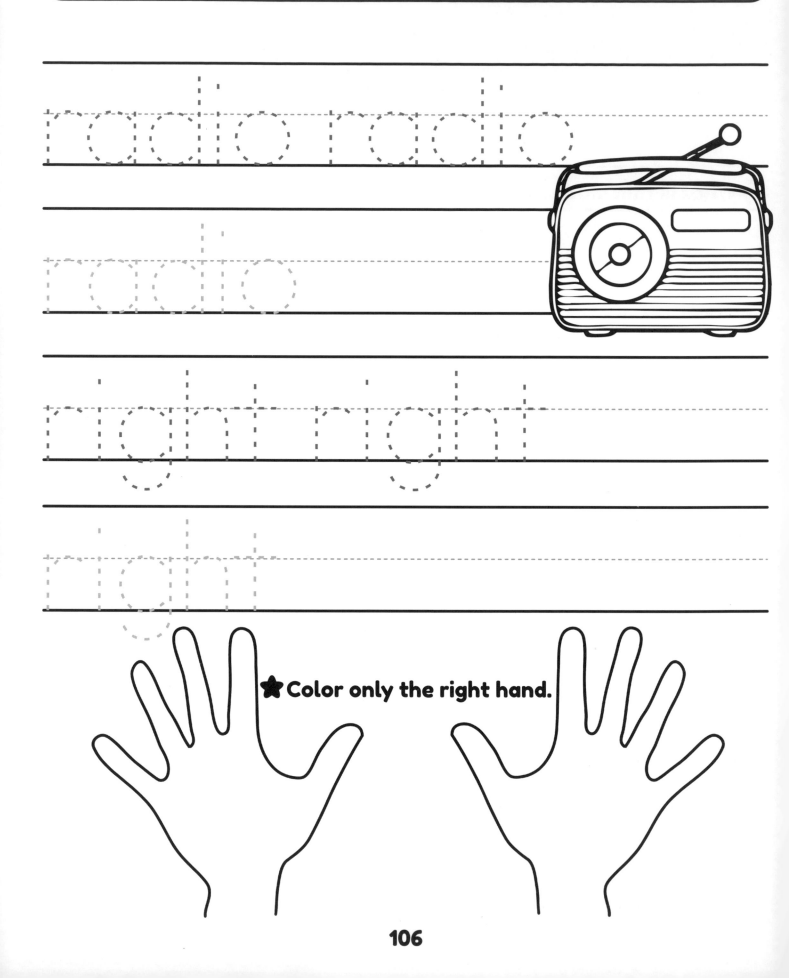

radio radio
radio

right right
right

★ Color only the right hand.

A B C D E F G H I J K L M N O P Q **R** S T U V W X Y Z

repair repair

repair

restaurant

restaurant

The table is set. Do you know the name of each item?

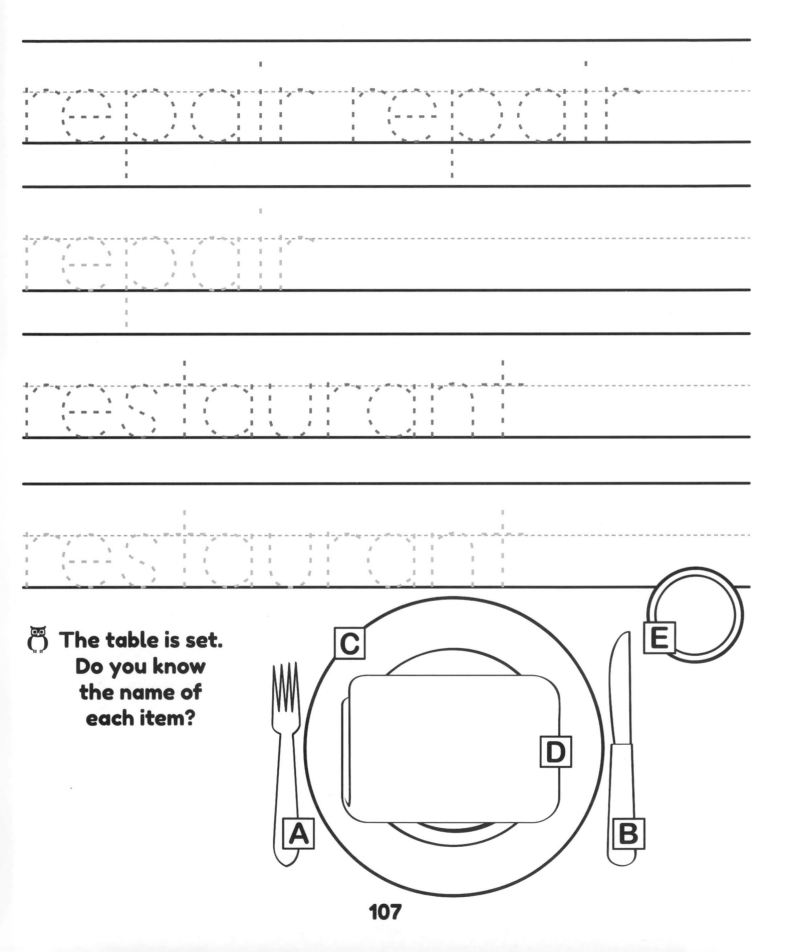

107

⭐ TRACE, WRITE, AND COLOR!

Ringo the rat
loves to listen
to rock music
on the
radio

🐻 CAN YOU WRITE THE LETTERS BY YOURSELF?

WRITE AND LEARN THE SIGHT WORDS.

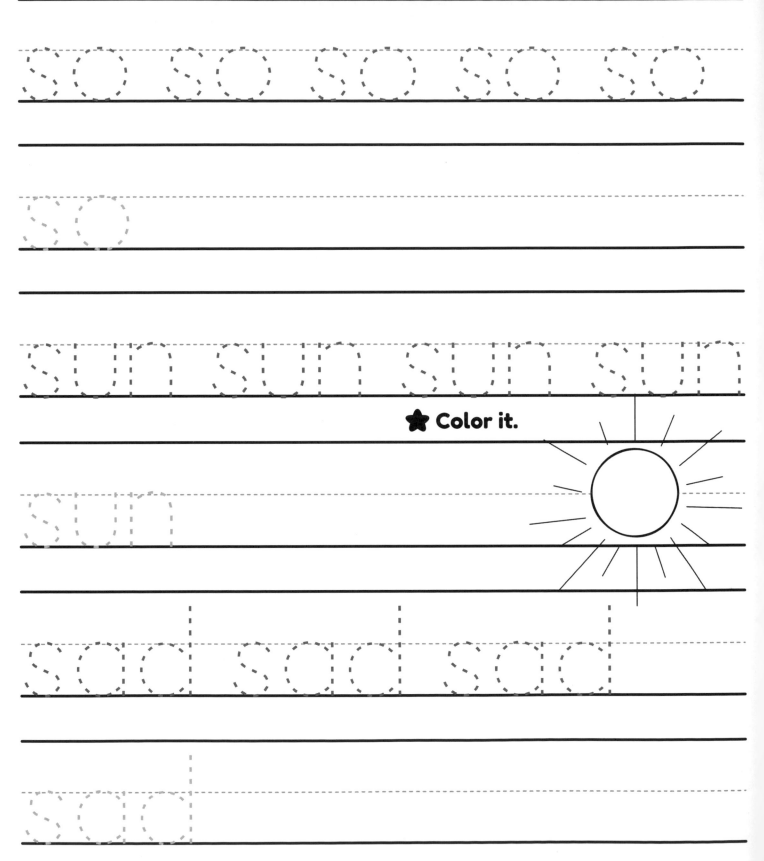

★ Color it.

say say say

say

see see

⭐ **What do you like seeing on TV?**

see

sea sea sea

sea

sky sky sky sky

sky

star star star

⭐ **Only color the stars.**

star

space space space

space

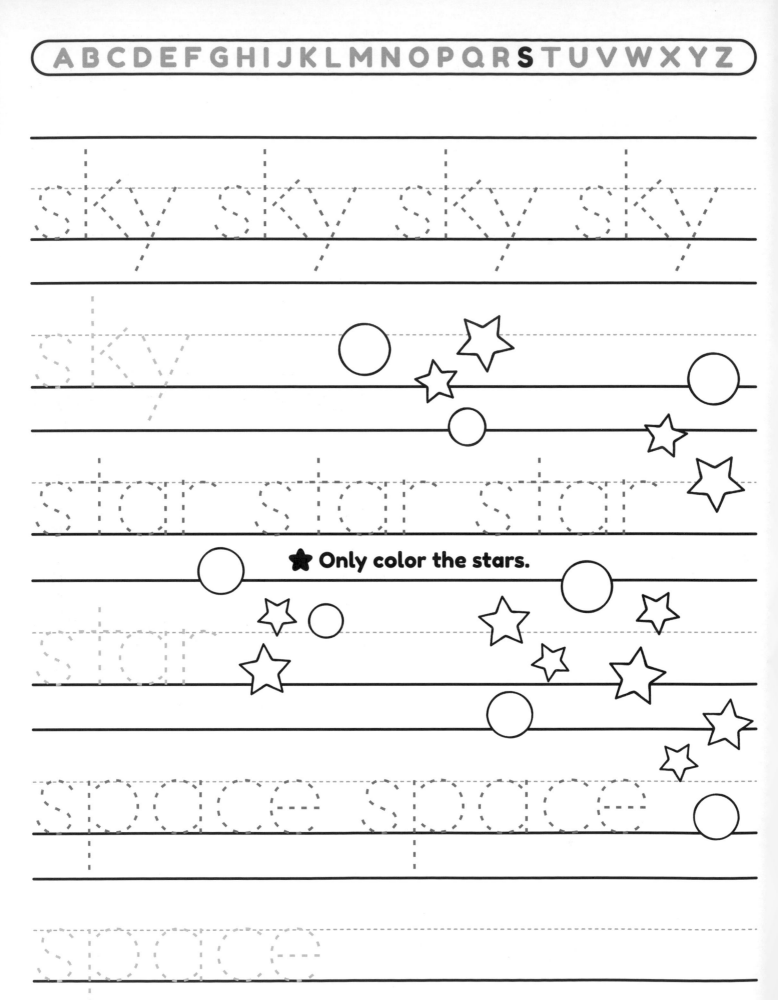

smile smile

smile

⭐ Try one of your own.

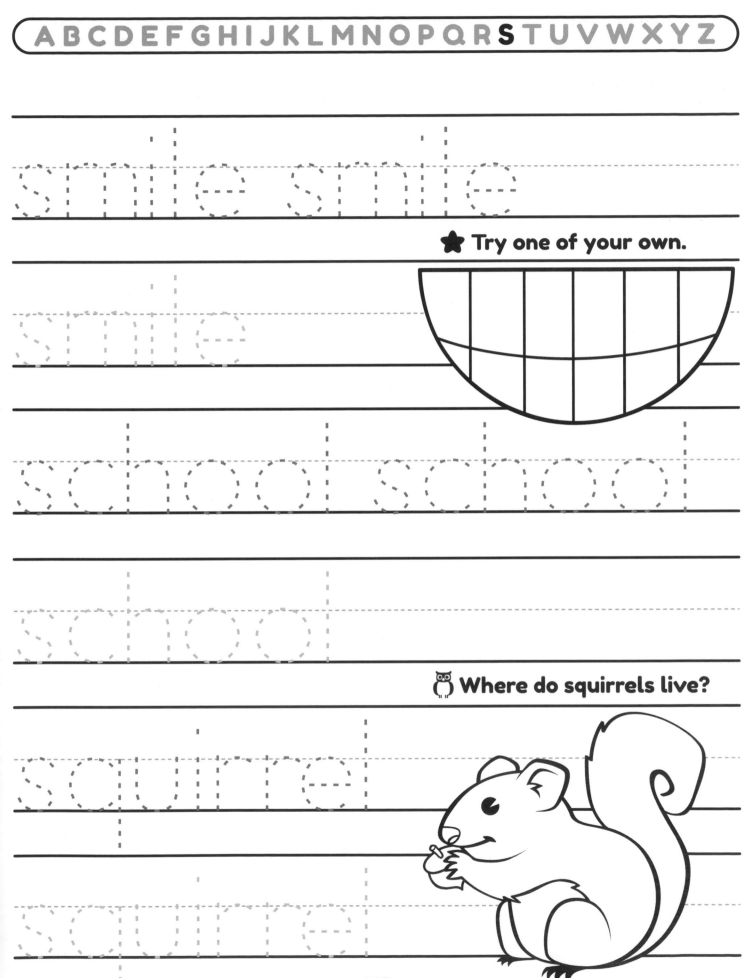

school school

school

🦉 Where do squirrels live?

squirrel

squirrel

113

A B C D E F G H I J K L M N O P Q R **S** T U V W X Y Z

⭐ TRACE, WRITE, AND COLOR!

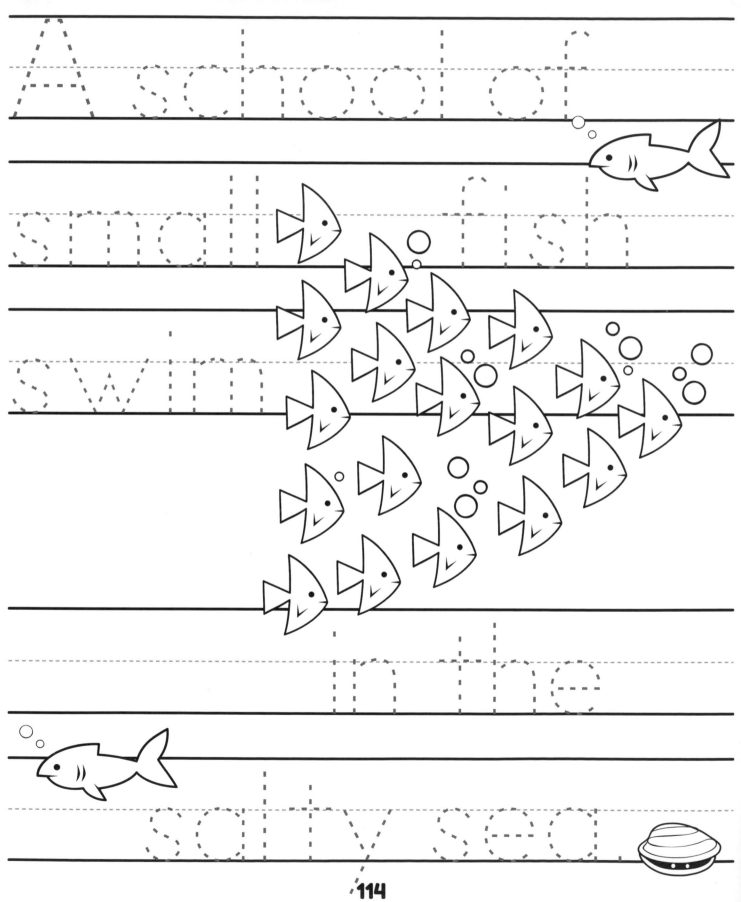

A school of

small fish

swim

in the

salty sea

114

CAN YOU WRITE THE LETTERS BY YOURSELF?

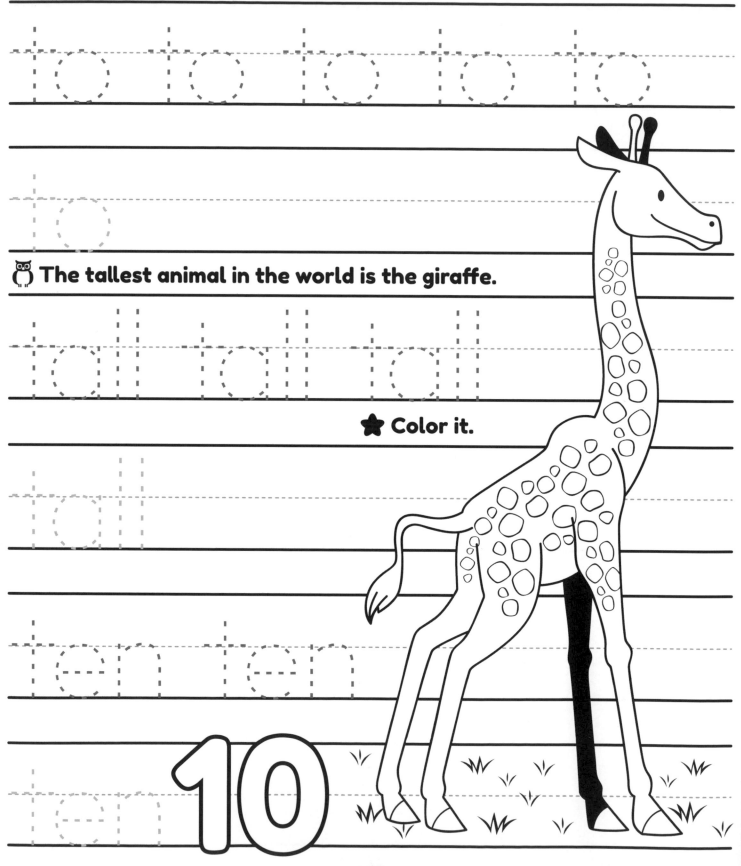

WRITE AND LEARN THE SIGHT WORDS.

to to to to to to
to

The tallest animal in the world is the giraffe.

tall tall tall

★ **Color it.**

tall

ten ten

10

ten

top top top

top

try try try try

try

toe toe toe

🦉 **How many toes do we have?**

toe

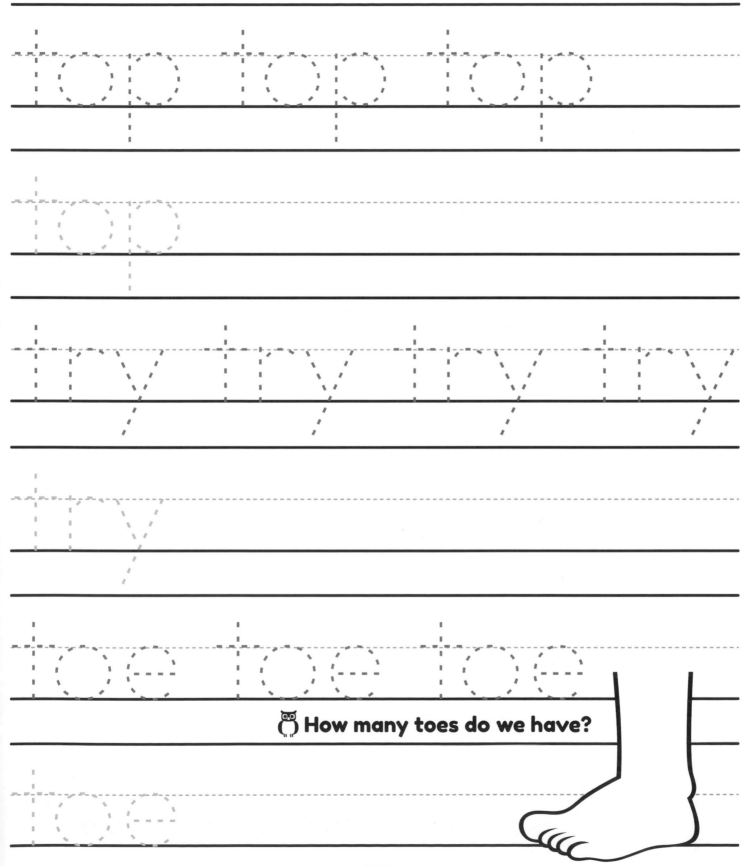

tool tool tool

tool

★ **Color the carpenter tools.**

tree tree tree

tree

train train

🦉 **Have you ever seen a train?**

train

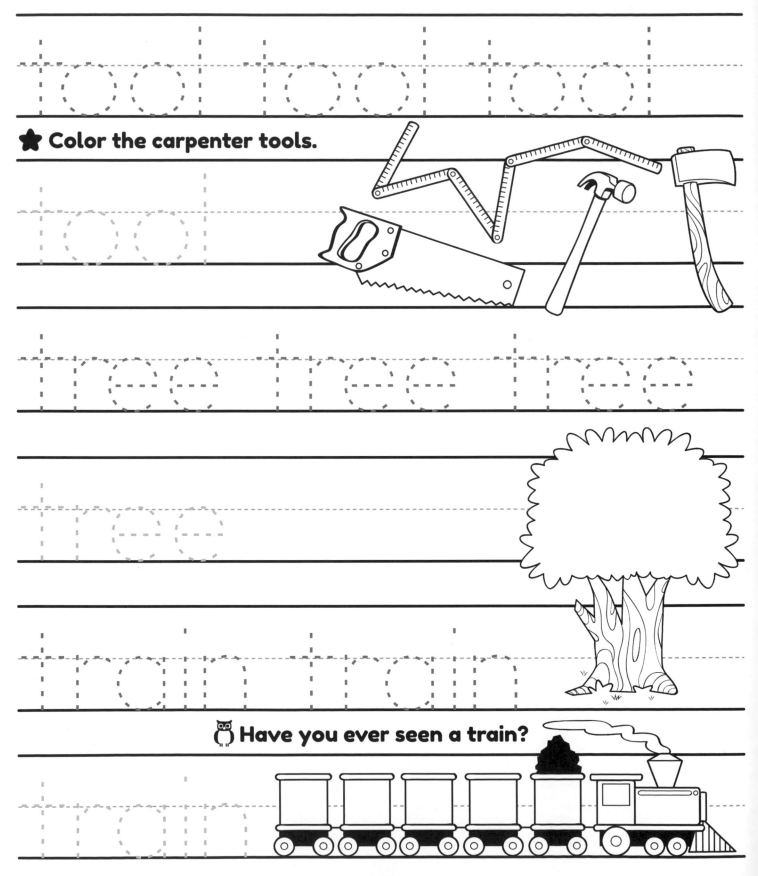

118

tomato tomato

tomato

⭐ **It's big and it's juicy. What color is it?**

turtle turtle

turtle

⭐ **Color the triangles only.**

triangle

triangle

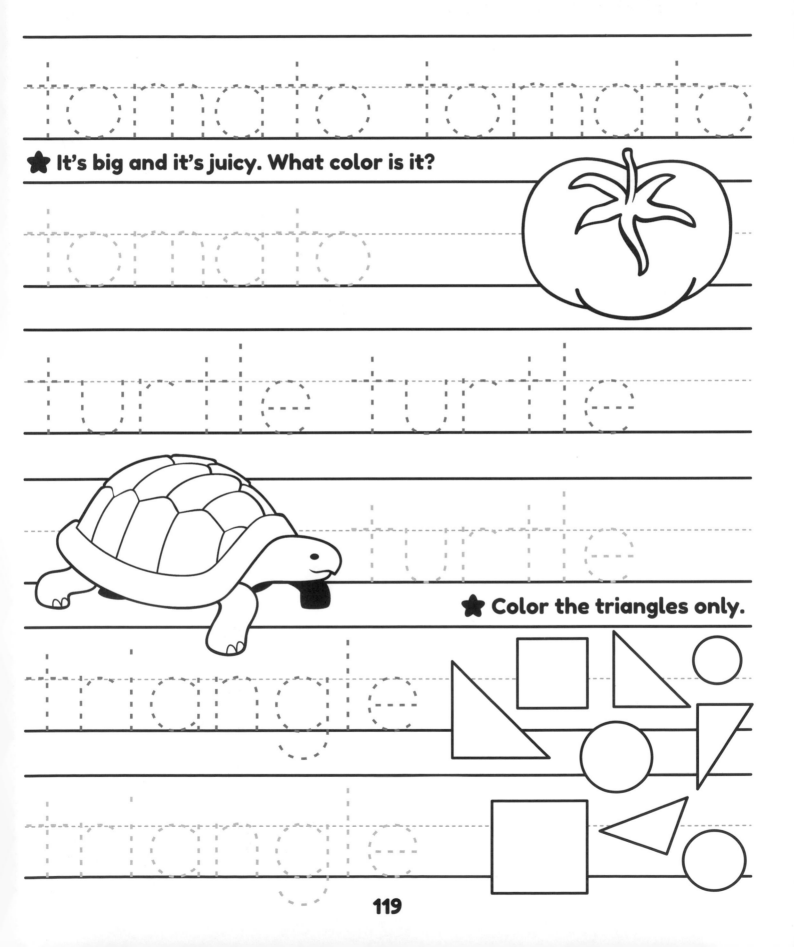

⭐ TRACE, WRITE, AND COLOR!

Tina the tall
giraffe
lost her
necktie
atop the
page

CAN YOU WRITE THE LETTERS BY YOURSELF?

WRITE AND LEARN THE SIGHT WORDS.

US US US US

US

up up up up

up

⭐ Can you draw the balloon going all the way up?

use use use

use

under under

under

usual usual

usual

uncle

⭐ **Can you draw your favorite uncle?**

uncle

ABCDEFGHIJKLMNOPQRSTUVWXYZ

until until until

until

united united

What does the U stand for?

U.S.A

united

ugly ugly ugly

ugly

124

⭐ **What does the horse need to become a unicorn? Draw it.**

unicorn

unicorn

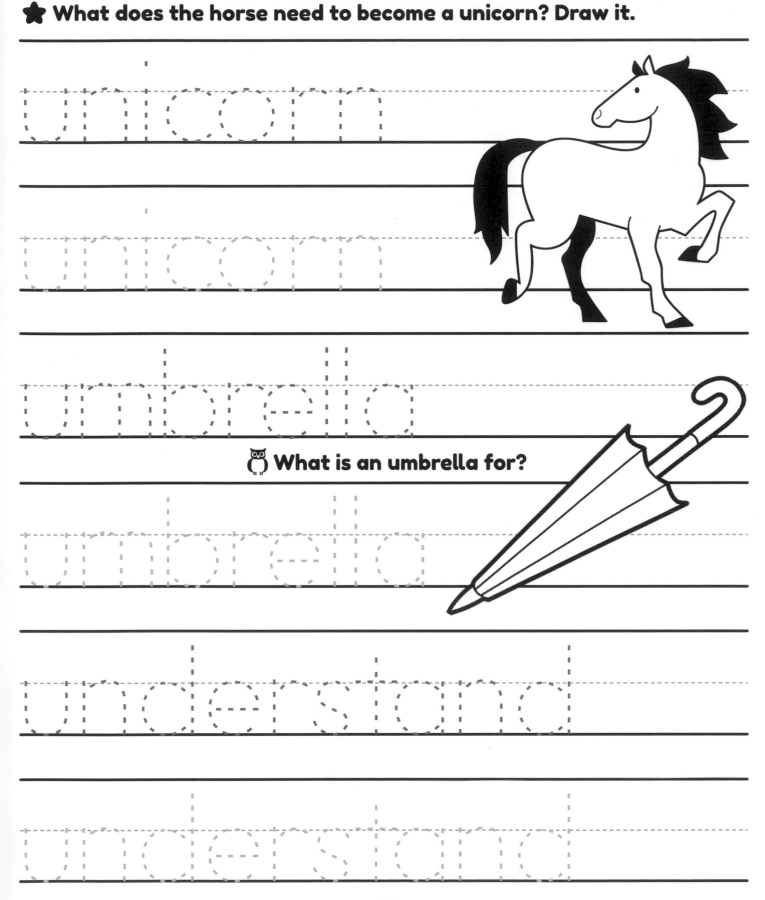

umbrella

🦉 **What is an umbrella for?**

umbrella

understand

understand

⭐ **TRACE, WRITE, AND COLOR!**

Some look

at a spider and

see this,

but others

see this.

There is no ugly.

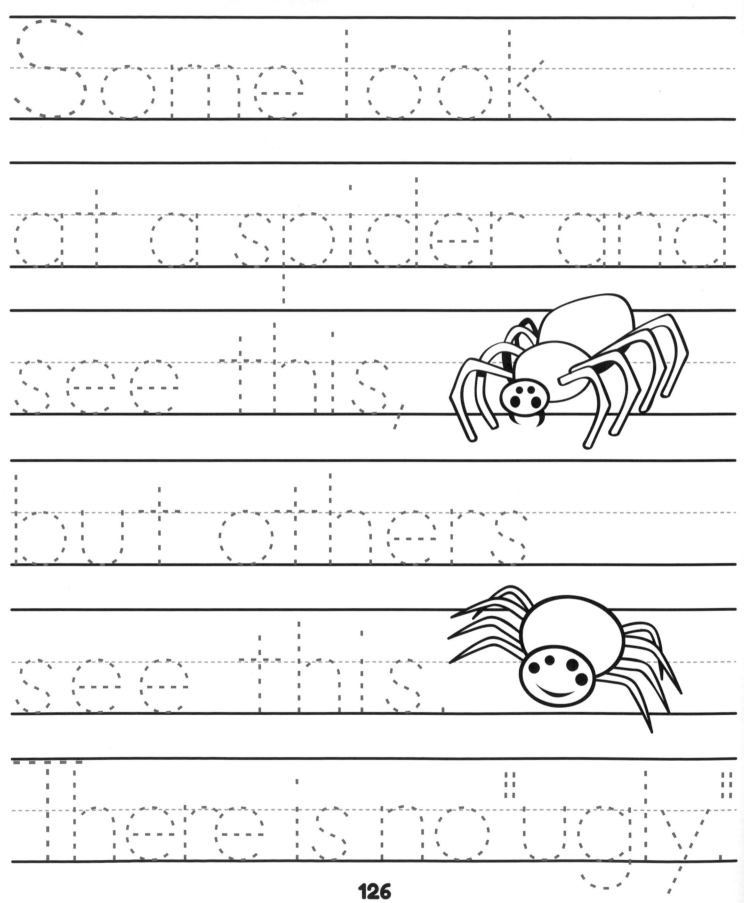

A B C D E F G H I J K L M N O P Q R S T U V W X Y Z

CAN YOU WRITE THE LETTERS BY YOURSELF?

WRITE AND LEARN THE SIGHT WORDS.

view view view

view

★ Draw the view from the window.

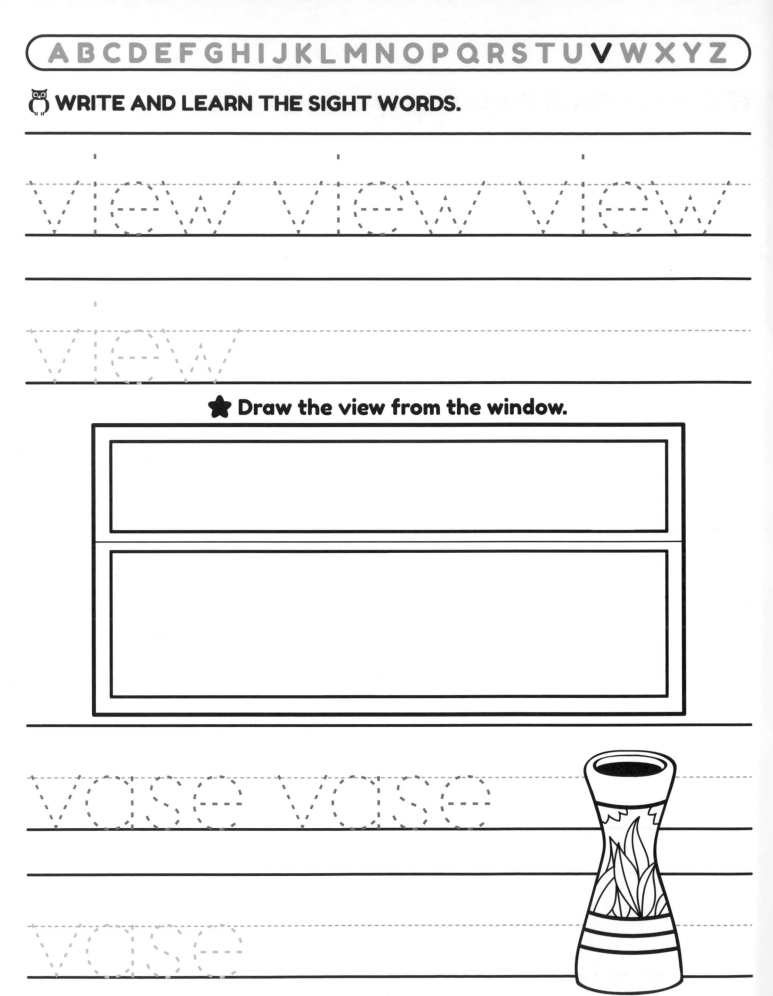

vase vase

vase

🦉 **Where do grapes come from?**

vine vine

vine

very very very

very

vain vain vain

vain

visit visit visit

visit

valley valley

valley

⭐ **Color the picture of the valley below.**

vehicle vehicle

vehicle

🦉 **Which one isn't a vehicle?**

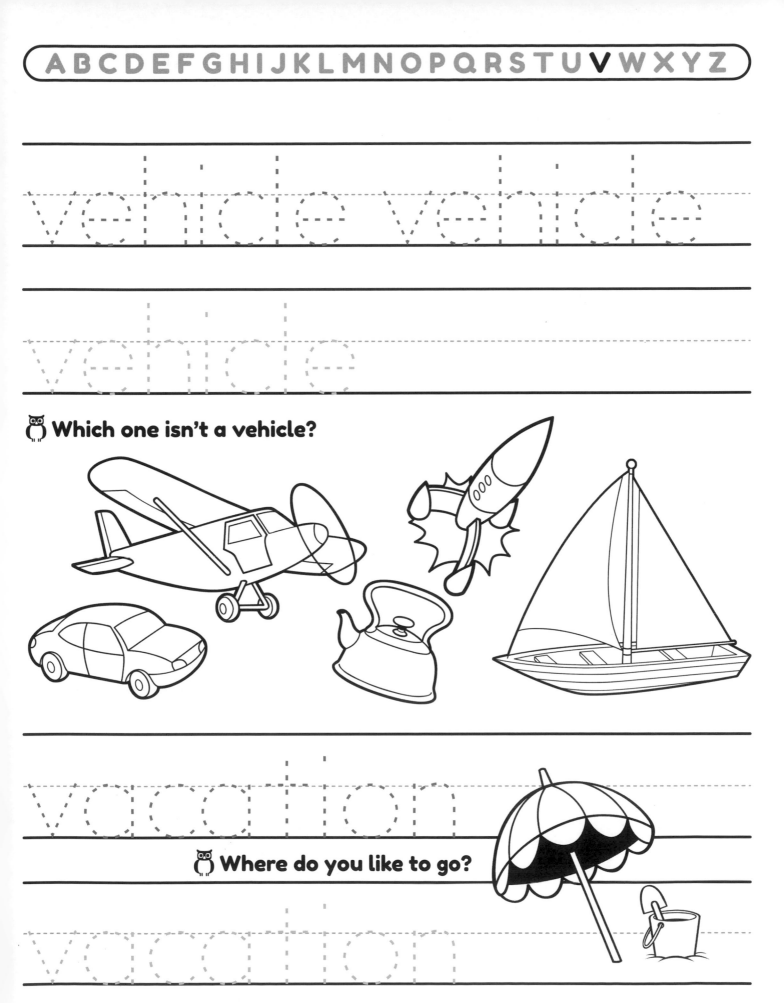

vacation

🦉 **Where do you like to go?**

vacation

⭐ TRACE, WRITE, AND COLOR!

There are two

volcanoes

in the valley

of dinosaurs.

CAN YOU WRITE THE LETTERS BY YOURSELF?

W   W   W   W

W   W   W   W

W   W   W   W   W

W   W   W   W   W

WRITE AND LEARN THE SIGHT WORDS.

we   we   we   we

we

way   way   way

way

⭐ Help her find the way home.

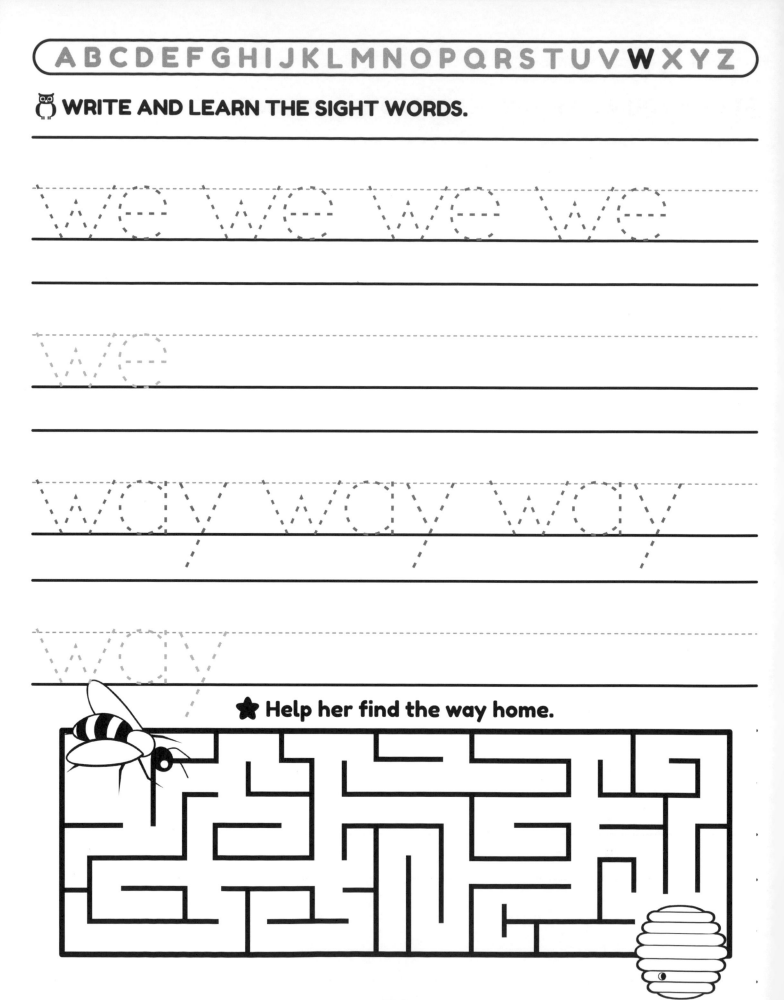

wet wet wet

wet

well well well

well

west west

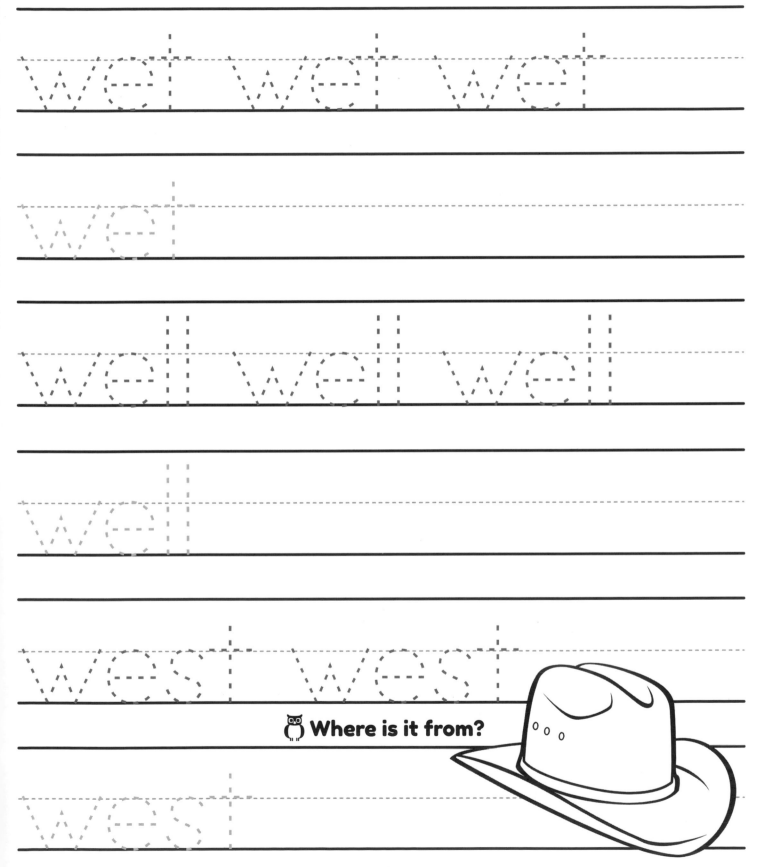

🦉 **Where is it from?**

west

wild wild wild

wild

wind wind wind

wind

white white

What color is the snowman?

white

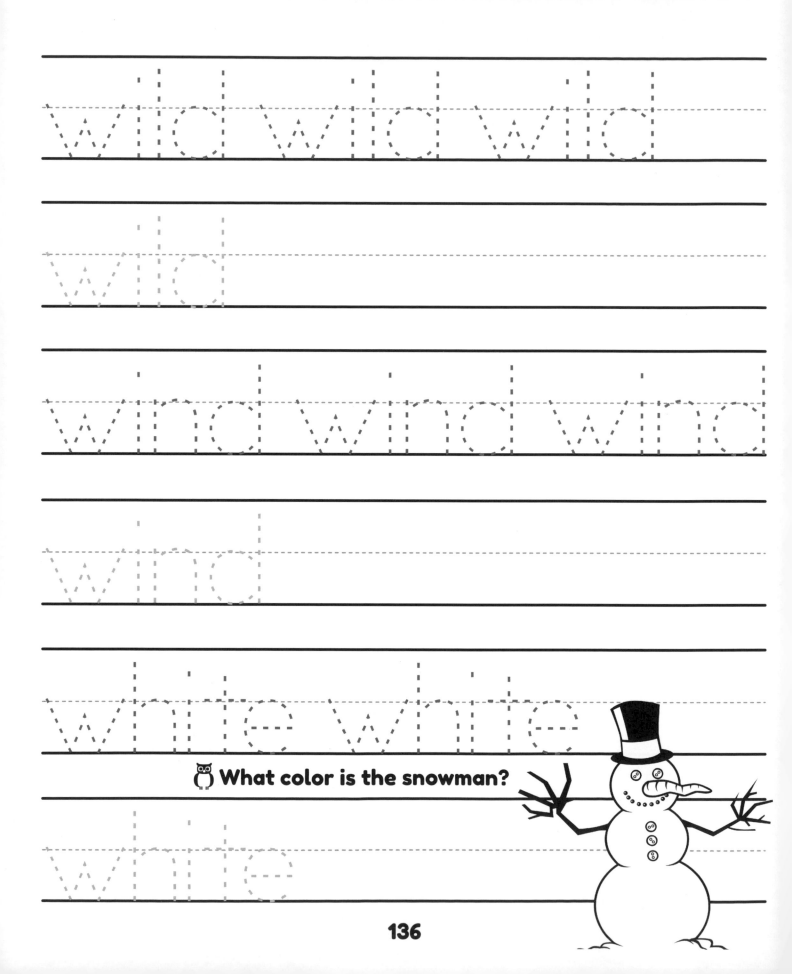

world world

world

★ **Color the Earth.**

write write

write

🦉 **What do you use a pencil for?**

woman woman

woman

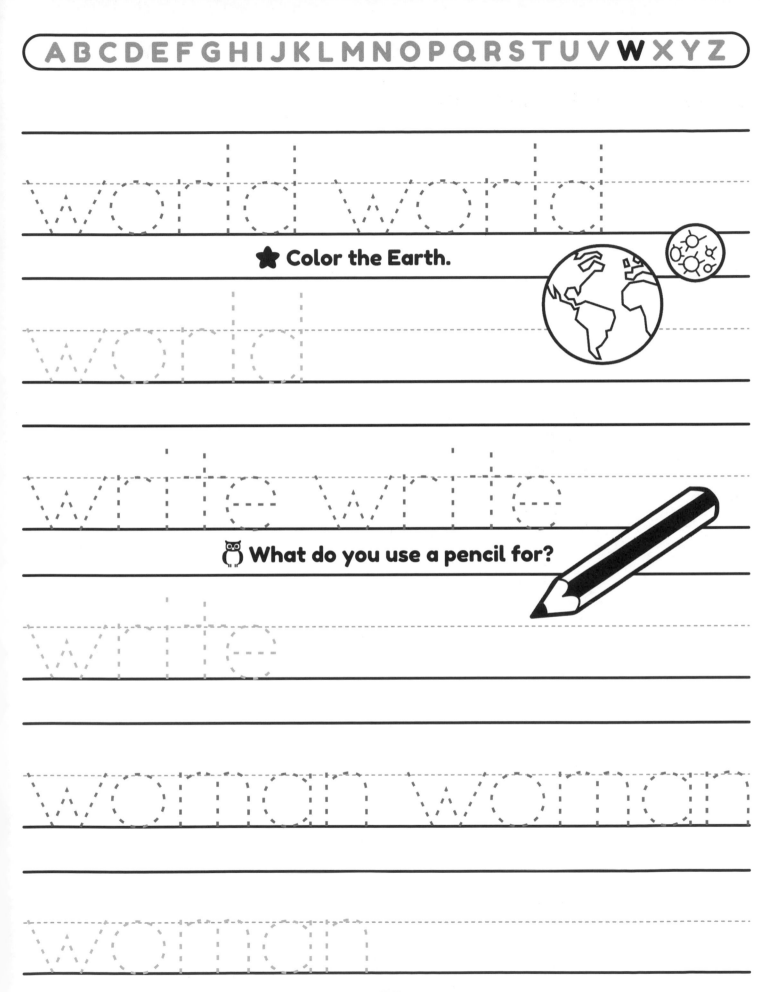

A B C D E F G H I J K L M N O P Q R S T U V **W** X Y Z

⭐ **TRACE, WRITE, AND COLOR!**

Willie White

the snowman

loves a windy

winter day

138

A B C D E F G H I J K L M N O P Q R S T U V W **X Y** Z

🧸 CAN YOU WRITE THE LETTERS BY YOURSELF?

CAN YOU WRITE THE LETTERS BY YOURSELF?

CAN YOU WRITE THE LETTERS BY YOURSELF?

ABCDEFGHIJKLMNOPQRSTUVW**XYZ**

WRITE AND LEARN THE SIGHT WORDS.

you you you

you

yes yes yes

yes

YES!

142

⭐ **Color the egg's yolk only.**

yolk yolk yolk

yolk

your your your

your

young young young

young

143

yellow yellow

yellow

⭐ **Color them yellow.**

yesterday

yesterday

ABCDEFGHIJKLMNOPQRSTUVW**XYZ**

zoo zoo zoo zoo

zoo

🦉 What animals live there?

zero zero

🦉 What letter does it look like?

0

zero

zebra

⭐ Draw her stripes.

zebra

145

⭐ TRACE, WRITE, AND COLOR!

This young

monkey loves

to play with

his yellow

yo-yo

at the zoo

A B C D E F G H I J K L M N O P Q R S T U V W X Y Z

★ BONUS ACTIVITY: Color by letter.

A = BLUE
B = GREEN
C = BROWN

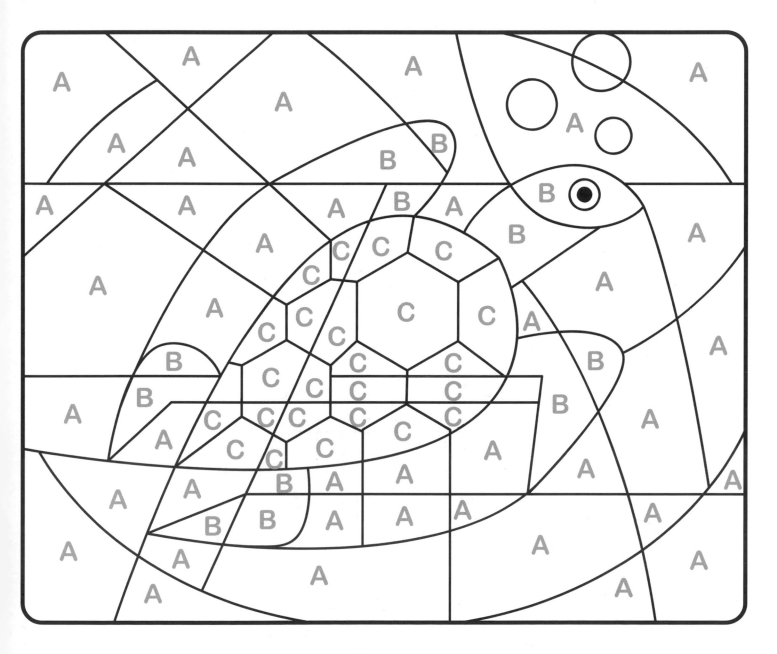

Solution

Turtle

A B C D E F G H I J K L M N O P Q R S T U V W X Y Z

★ **BONUS ACTIVITY: Connect the dots and color.**

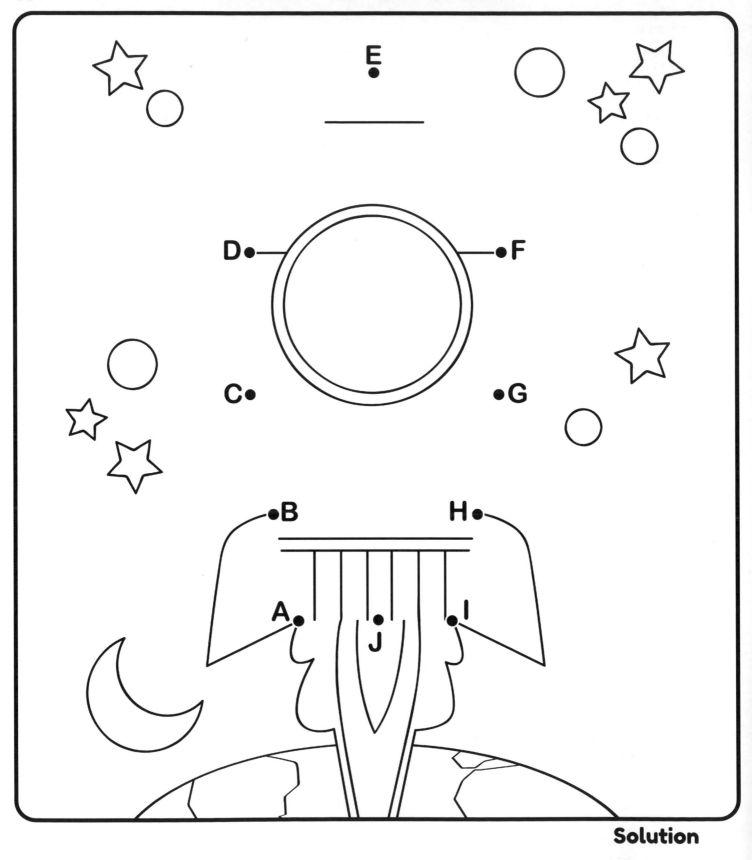

Solution

Rocket

A B C D E F G H I J K L M N O P Q R S T U V W X Y Z

⭐ **BONUS ACTIVITY: Can you trace each figure with a single stroke?**

A B C D E F G H I J K L M N O P Q R S T U V W X Y Z

★ **BONUS ACTIVITY: Find and circle each sight word from the list.**

◆ are ◆ ball ◆ ear ◆ get ◆ joy ◆ may ◆ once ◆ pair ◆ sky

A B C D E F G H I J K L M N O P Q R S T U V W X Y Z

⭐ BONUS ACTIVITY: Picture crossword.

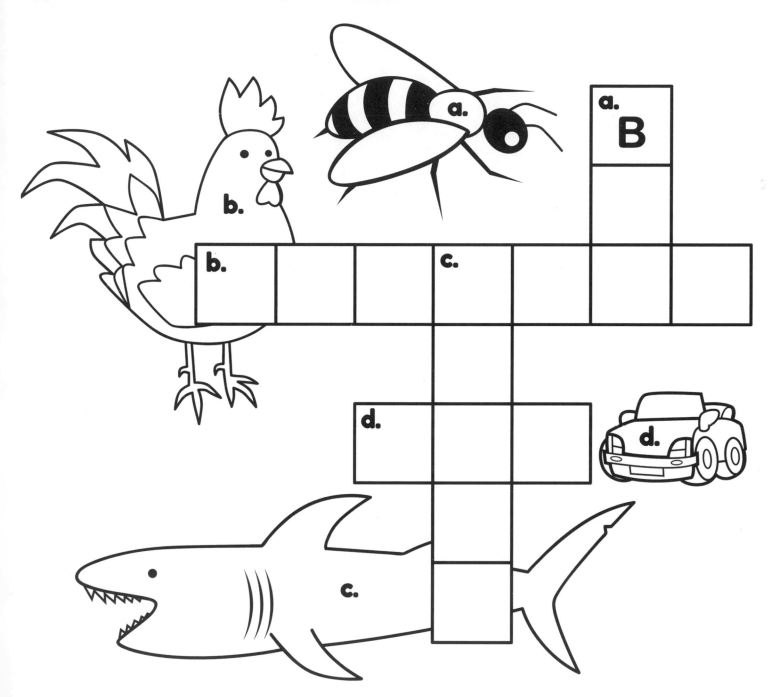

Solution

a. Bee
b. Rooster
c. Shark
d. Car

A B C D E F G H I J K L M N O P Q R S T U V W X Y Z

★ BONUS ACTIVITY: Trace the bowling ball spins to hit the pins.

⭐ BONUS ACTIVITY: Picture crossword.

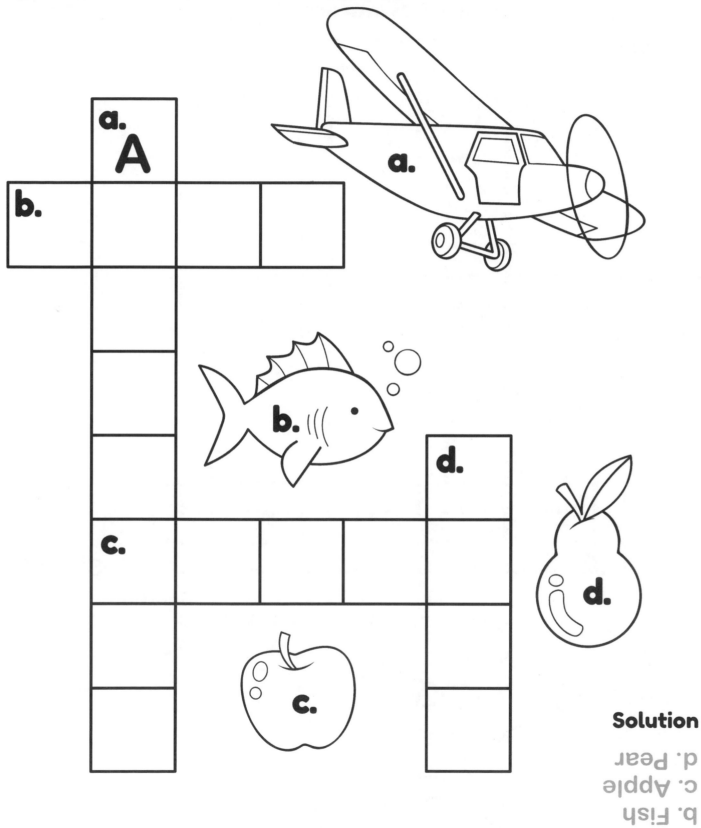

a.

b.

c.

d.

a. A

Solution

a. Airplane
b. Fish
c. Apple
d. Pear

A B C D E F G H I J K L M N O P Q R S T U V W X Y Z

⭐ **BONUS ACTIVITY:** Find the way out of the maze to combine both sight words into one.

sea

shells

Solution

shells

sea

★ BONUS ACTIVITY: Complete the tongue twister with the right word.

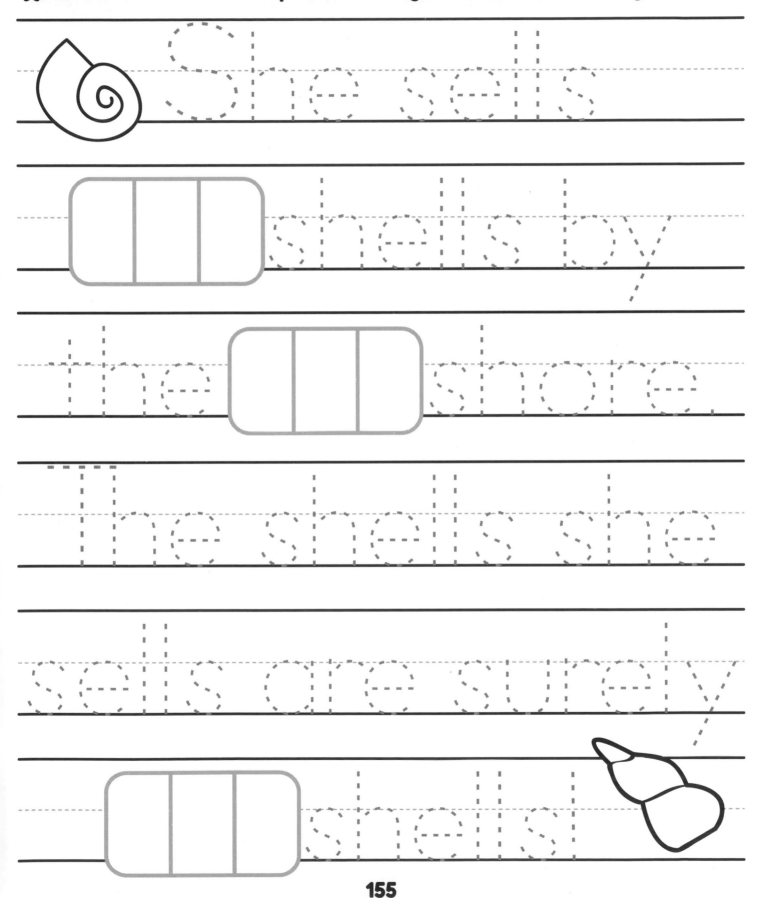

She sells

_____ shells by

the _____ shore

The shells she

sells are surely

_____ shells!

⭐ **BONUS ACTIVITY: Sight word search.**

```
K I N G G O Y J S M J
S T A Y R A T S U C O
V G R M W A I R E I Y
D Y O E D K S K Y T K
T A U G A C I S F Y C
L Z N G Y L J E R W H
E O D C A Z U G U M A
L C V V E L W Y I G S
B E E E B W N W T A E
U N I T E D S O P M Q
D A W N T R E E W E U
```

Solution

A B C D E F G H I J K L M N O P Q R S T U V W X Y Z

AFTER COMPLETING EACH PAGE, COLOR A STAR TO TRACK HOW MUCH YOU HAVE DONE.

73 74 75 76 77 78 79 80

81 82 83 84 85 86 87 88

89 90 91 92 93 94 95 96

97 98 99 100 101 102 103 104

105 106 107 108 109 110 111 112

113 114 115 116 117 118 119 120

121 122 123 124 125 126 127 128

129 130 131 132 133 134 135 136

137 138 139 140 141 142 143 144

145 146 147 148 149 150 151 152

153 154 155 156

158

A B C D E F G H I J K L M N O P Q R S T U V W X Y Z

🦉 LIST OF ALL SIGHT WORDS INCLUDED IN THIS BOOK

a	count	garden	is
above	country	get	island
again	dance	gift	it
all	dawn	giraffe	jacket
always	desk	girls	jar
am	did	give	jelly
and	dinosaurs	glad	job
answer	do	go	join
ant	doctor	grandma	joy
apple	does	grandmother	juice
are	dog	grape	jump
around	doll	grass	jungle
ask	draw	green	just
at	duck	grew	keep
aunt	each	grow	kettle
back	ear	hair	key
ball	early	happily	kick
be	earth	happy	kind
beans	eat	have	king
bee	egg	he	kiss
begin	elephant	hen	kitchen
below	end	her	kite
big	even	him	knee
bird	evening	himself	know
blue	every	home	last
boat	face	honey	late
both	feet	horse	learn
brown	few	hot	left
but	find	how	less
cabbage	fish	ice	let
cake	fly	icecream	light
can	for	idea	like
car	fork	if	listen
cat	found	important	little
chase	freedom	in	log
city	friends	inside	long
close	frog	into	look
coffee	fruit	invent	lost
color	game	iron	love

man	park	seashells	ugly
mane	patch	seashore	umbrella
many	pay	see	uncle
map	pencil	seed	under
may	penguin	seen	understand
maze	people	shark	unicorn
me	pig	sixth	united
meat	pigpen	sky	until
mice	pineapple	small	up
milk	pink	smile	us
moonlight	plane	snowman	use
morning	play	so	usual
mother	pour	some	vacation
mud	quack	space	valley
music	quarter	spider	vase
my	queen	squirrel	vehicle
name	quest	star	very
nature	question	stay	view
near	quick	sun	vine
necktie	quiet	sure	visit
need	quit	swim	volcanoes
new	quite	swimming	was
nice	quiz	tall	way
nine	rabbits	ten	we
no	radio	the	well
now	rain	their	west
number	rat	there	wet
ocean	reading	these	while
of	real	this	white
off	red	tasty	wild
on	repair	to	wind
once	restaurant	toe	windy
one	right	tomato	winter
open	ring	tool	with
or	rock	top	woman
orca	run	train	won't
others	sad	tree	world
owl	salty	triangle	write
page	say	try	yellow
paint	school	turtle	yes
pair	sea	two	yesterday

A B C D E F G H I J K L M N O P Q R S T U V W X Y Z

yolk
you
young
your
zebra
zero
zoo

🦉 ABOUT THE AUTHOR

Diego Jourdan Pereira is an author of puzzle and activity books with a background in illustration, comic-books, and graphic design. In addition to his own volumes for children and adults, he has worked on licensed properties such as Teenage Mutant Ninja Turtles, Transformers, Donald Duck, Grumpy Cat, LEGO, Mars Attacks!, Regular Show, Sesame Street, Star Wars, Toy Story, and WWE, for an international clientele including DC Comics, DC Thomson Media, Dover Publications, IDW Publishing, Skyhorse Publishing, and The Topps Company.

IF YOU LOVED THIS BOOK DON'T MISS THE
GIANT BOOK OF GAMES AND PUZZLES FOR SMART KIDS
HOURS OF FUN FOR THE WHOLE FAMILY!

DIEGO JOURDAN PEREIRA
GIANT BOOK OF GAMES AND PUZZLES FOR SMART KIDS
MORE THAN 1000 FUN AND EDUCATIONAL ACTIVITIES